# A Presidential Scrapbook

Written by Joel King

DECLARATION-OF-INDEPENDENCE

Edited by Jordan C. King
Published by Bramley Books

## To my parents, Joe and Margaret King, for inspiring my love for history.

Find more fun and educational resources by Joel King at www.BramleyBooks.com.
Cover Design by Cathi Stevenson

A Presidential Scrapbook, Joel F. King  © 2011

ISBN 978-1-932786-43-9

# Table of Contents

## How to play the President Quiz game:

Start on page 6 and choose a trivia question.  Take a guess at the answer, then turn to that page to see if you are correct.  Continue by following another quiz question until you arrive back on George Washington's page.  You are finished and can start again!

# Who can be president?

According to Article II of the U.S. Constitution, the president of the United States must:

- be a natural born citizen of the United States
- be at least thirty-five years old
- have been a permanent resident in the United States for at least fourteen years

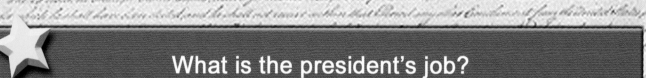

# What is the president's job?

The U.S. government is comprised of three branches. The legislative branch consists of the Senate and the House of Representatives. Together, the Senate and House is called Congress and their primary task is to write laws. The judicial branch consists of the federal courts and the Supreme Court. Their primary job is to interpret the law. The executive branch is made up of the president, the vice president, and others who help the president. Their primary job is to execute the law.

As head of the excutive branch, the president has a lot of powers and responsibilities. The president:

- can sign or veto legislation
- is commander-in-chief and commands the military
- takes care that the laws are faithfully executed
- appoints Ambassadors and federal officers
- nominates federal judges
- can grant pardons and reprieves

# The Presidential Oath

I do solemnly swear that I will faithfully execute the office of the President of the United States, and will, to the best of my ability, preserve, protect, and defend the Constitution of the United States.

# Index of the Presidents

| Number | Name | Birth State | Term in Office |
|---|---|---|---|
| 1 | George Washington | Virginia | 1789 - 1797 |
| 2 | John Adams | Massachusetts | 1797 - 1801 |
| 3 | Thomas Jefferson | Virginia | 1801 - 1809 |
| 4 | James Madison | Virginia | 1809 - 1817 |
| 5 | James Monroe | Virginia | 1817 - 1825 |
| 6 | John Quincy Adams | Massachusetts | 1825 - 1829 |
| 7 | Andrew Jackson | South Carolina | 1829 - 1837 |
| 8 | Martin Van Buren | New York | 1837 - 1841 |
| 9 | William Henry Harrison | Virginia | 1841 |
| 10 | John Tyler | Virginia | 1841 - 1845 |
| 11 | James K. Polk | North Carolina | 1845 - 1849 |
| 12 | Zachary Taylor | Virginia | 1849 - 1850 |
| 13 | Millard Fillmore | New York | 1850 - 1853 |
| 14 | Franklin Pierce | New Hampshire | 1853 - 1857 |
| 15 | James Buchanan | Pennsylvania | 1857 - 1861 |
| 16 | Abraham Lincoln | Kentucky | 1861 - 1865 |
| 17 | Andrew Johnson | North Carolina | 1865 - 1869 |
| 18 | Ulysses S. Grant | Ohio | 1869 - 1877 |
| 19 | Rutherford B. Hayes | Ohio | 1877 - 1881 |
| 20 | James A. Garfield | Ohio | 1881 |
| 21 | Chester A. Arthur | Vermont | 1881 - 1885 |
| 22 | Grover Cleveland | New Jersey | 1885 - 1889 |
| 23 | Benjamin Harrison | Ohio | 1889 - 1893 |
| 24 | Grover Cleveland | New Jersey | 1893 - 1897 |
| 25 | William McKinley | Ohio | 1897 - 1901 |
| 26 | Theodore Roosevelt | New York | 1901 - 1909 |
| 27 | William H. Taft | Ohio | 1909 - 1913 |
| 28 | Woodrow Wilson | Virginia | 1913 - 1921 |
| 29 | Warren G. Harding | Ohio | 1921 - 1923 |
| 30 | Calvin Coolidge | Vermont | 1923 - 1929 |
| 31 | Herbert Hoover | Iowa | 1929 - 1933 |
| 32 | Franklin D. Roosevelt | New York | 1933 - 1945 |
| 33 | Harry S. Truman | Missouri | 1945 - 1953 |
| 34 | Dwight D. Eisenhower | Texas | 1953 - 1961 |
| 35 | John F. Kennedy | Massachusetts | 1961 - 1963 |
| 36 | Lyndon B. Johnson | Texas | 1963 - 1969 |
| 37 | Richard M. Nixon | California | 1969 - 1974 |
| 38 | Gerald R. Ford | Nebraska | 1974 - 1977 |
| 39 | James "Jimmy" Carter | Georgia | 1977 - 1981 |
| 40 | Ronald Reagan | Illinois | 1981 - 1989 |
| 41 | George H. W. Bush | Massachusetts | 1989 - 1993 |
| 42 | William Jefferson "Bill" Clinton | Arkansas | 1993 - 2001 |
| 43 | George Walker Bush | Connecticut | 2001 - 2009 |
| 44 | Barack Obama | Hawaii | 2009 - present |

# #1 George Washington
## (1789 - 1797)

George Washington was born in Virginia when Virginia was still an English colony. When he was young, Washington became a surveyor and a soldier in the English army. Over time, he (like many colonists) became tired of being ruled by a king and wanted America to be independent.

When the colonies finally decided to break free from English rule, Washington (who was general of the Continental Army) was chosen to lead the cause. The ensuing war was tough and lasted seven years, but through General Washington's leadership, the colonists won their freedom in 1783.

Though Washington became a hero, he didn't try to capitalize on his popularity. Instead, he returned to his farm in Virginia. A few years later, however, his country needed his services one more time. His country needed a president!

Born: February 22, 1732
Died: December 14, 1799

After the U.S. Constitution became the law of the land, Americans needed to select a president that they could trust and they chose George Washington! President Washington served four years and was re-elected for a second term. After his second term ended, he returned to his home in Virginia.

John Adams was Washington's chief opponent in both elections. In those days, Adams became America's vice president because he received the second-most votes.

General Washington in command during the Revolutionary War.

| 1776 | 1783 | 1788 | 1789 |
|------|------|------|------|
| America declares its independence from England | America wins the Revolutionary War | George Washington is elected America's first president! | Washington is sworn in as America's first president |

In this famous painting, George Washington and the Continental Army are crossing the Delaware River during the Revolutionary War.

George Washington is often called the "Father" of our country. He is one of the four presidents featured on Mount Rushmore.

## PRESIDENT QUIZ

### WHO AM I?

1801 – 1809

Page 10

### TRIVIA

Who was president during the Civil War?

Page 36

"If the freedom of speech is taken away then dumb and silent we may be led, like sheep to a slaughter."

— George Washington

| 1790 | 1790 | 1796 | 1797 |
|---|---|---|---|
| The U.S. capital is moved from New York City to Philadelphia | The U.S. Census counts 3.9 million Americans | America takes control of Detroit from the British | Washington retires to Virginia after serving his last term |

# #2   John Adams
## (1797 - 1801)

John Adams, the oldest of three sons, was born in 1735 in what is now Quincy, Massachusetts. At the age of sixteen, he went to Harvard College. He became a school teacher after he graduated and then a successful lawyer. In 1764, he married Abigail Smith and, together, the two had six children.

Born: October 30, 1735
Died: July 4, 1826

In 1770, John Adams became the lawyer for a number of British soldiers who were being tried for murder after they fired upon American colonists in what is called "The Boston Massacre". Despite local anger toward the soldiers, Adams saved all the men on trial from the hangman's rope. Hard feelings for Adams didn't last long because, a few years later, Massachusetts chose him as one of its representatives to the first and second Continental Congresses!

The incident known as the "Boston Massacre" led to the deaths of five colonists.

John Adams served as George Washington's vice president during Washington's two terms. When Washington retired, the country cast ballots for a new president and Adams was its pick. Shortly after Adams took office, our nation was thrust into a "quasi-war" with France. President Adams and many U.S. leaders feared a French invasion and built up the army and navy, but France didn't attack American soil and the United States remained safe.

| 1797 | 1797 | 1798 | 1799 |
|---|---|---|---|
| John Adams takes office as new president | "Old Ironsides" sets sail to defend America | American quasi-war with France begins | In France, Napoleon overthrows his nation's Executive Directory |

By 1796, France and Great Britain were engaged in a war that had been going on for nearly ten years. Shortly after John Adams took office in 1797, France began capturing American ships because France saw America as a British ally. Neither the U.S. or France officially declared war on the other, thus a "quasi-war" broke out.

———————

Did you know that John Adams is considered one of America's *Founding Fathers*?

In 1776, he was the foremost debater in trying to get the "Declaration of Independence" adopted by the Continental Congress.

...and he signed it too!

The USS *Constitution* (or "Old Ironsides") was christened on October 21, 1797, when John Adams was president. The 44-gun, three-masted frigate would sail into history, defeating five British warships in the War of 1812.

Today, the USS *Constitution* is still officially on active duty, easily making the ship the oldest commissioned vessel in the U.S. Navy.

## PRESIDENT QUIZ

### WHO AM I?

1961 - 1963

Page 74

### TRIVIA

Who was the first African-American president?

Page 92

"Remember, democracy never lasts long. It soon wastes, exhausts, and murders itself. There never was a democracy yet that did not commit suicide."

— John Adams

| 1799 | 1800 | 1800 | 1801 |
|---|---|---|---|
| George Washington dies in Virginia | The first vaccination in the U.S. against small pox is administered | The U.S. Census counts 5.3 million Americans | Washington, D.C., becomes the new U.S. capital |

# Thomas Jefferson
## (1801 - 1809)

Thomas Jefferson was born in 1743 in Virginia. He was the third of ten children. When he was fourteen years old, his father died and young Thomas inherited 5,000 acres of land and dozens of slaves. In 1772, he married Martha Wayles Skelton. The two had six children together. Tragically, one child died at birth.

Jefferson became the primary author of the Declaration of Independence. The document was written in 1776 and stated that the thirteen colonies were finished with being ruled by the British and were now free to govern as they pleased. Of course, England was outraged with the colonists and the Revolutionary War soon began.

Born: April 13, 1743
Died: July 4, 1826

Thomas Jefferson became president in 1801 by beating John Adams in one of the most disputed elections in U.S. history. Four years later, he was elected to a second term. During Jefferson's presidency, the U.S. made the "Louisiana Purchase" from France and fought the First Barbary War against pirates in northern Africa. Jefferson retired after his second term ended in 1809.

The United States nearly doubled in size when it made the "Louisiana Purchase" from France for 15 million dollars. Over time, the United States would expand to reach the Pacific Coast.

| 1801 | 1801 | 1803 | 1804 |
|---|---|---|---|
| Thomas Jefferson takes office as new president | The First Barbary War begins | The U.S. makes the "Louisiana Purchase" from France | Napoleon becomes the Emperor of France |

In the Election of 1800, Jefferson's political party was so confident of victory over President John Adams that it selected two candidates to run (Thomas Jefferson and Aaron Burr). But when the votes were cast and the electoral college met to select a winner, the unthinkable happened. Jefferson and Burr were tied with 73 votes each! According to the Constitution, if there was a tie, the U.S. House of Representatives would have to meet and vote for a winner. And vote they did! Thirty-five times the House voted and each time Jefferson and Burr got the same number of votes. Finally, in the thirty-sixth vote, Federalist Alexander Hamilton broke party ranks and cast the deciding vote for Jefferson. Jefferson became president and, thanks to Hamilton, Aaron Burr had to settle with being vice president.

In 1804, Aaron Burr and Alexander Hamilton dueled each other in New Jersey. Hamilton shot first and missed. Burr, who was still vice president at the time, returned fire. His musket ball struck Hamilton in the lower abdomen and, a few moments later, Hamilton died. The duel stemmed from the 1800 Presidential Election and was legal at that time.

Did you know that Thomas Jefferson and John Adams died on the same day? The date was July 4th, 1826.

Hamilton and Burr prepare to duel in New Jersey.

## PRESIDENT QUIZ

### WHO AM I?

2009 -

Page 92

### TRIVIA

Which president was assassinated in Dallas, Texas?

Page 74

"I predict future happiness for Americans if they can prevent the government from wasting the labors of the people under the pretense of taking care of them."

— Thomas Jefferson

| 1805 | 1806 | 1807 | 1808 |
|---|---|---|---|
| Lewis and Clark begin their expedition of the West | Zebulon Pike begins his expedition of the Southwest | Former VP Aaron Burr found not guilty of treason | Congress prohibits the importing of African slaves |

# James Madison
## (1809 - 1817)

James Madison, the oldest of twelve children, was born in Virginia in 1751. In his youth, he studied under a Scottish teacher and a reverend. In 1769, he began studies at what is now Princeton University and graduated two years later. Madison was only twenty-five years old when the Revolutionary War began. He served in the Virginia state legislature for most of the war and became a friend of Thomas Jefferson.

Born: March 16, 1751
Died: June 28, 1836

James Madison was president during the War of 1812.

After the Revolutionary War, Madison became more active as an American politician and political philosopher. He was the principal author of the U.S. Constitution and a key architect of the "Bill of Rights". Because of this, he is often called both the "Father of the Constitution" and the "Father of the Bill of Rights".

Madison's work was appreciated by many and he was chosen by President Jefferson to be America's Secretary of State. He served in this position until the end of Jefferson's final term in office and his popularity continued to grow.

After Jefferson retired, James Madison ran for president in 1808 and won. He also won again four years later. During his tenure as Commander in Chief, he had to deal with one of the most trying times in U.S. history, the War of 1812. Battles against the British were fought in Canada, the Atlantic Ocean, the Gulf of Mexico, and on American soil. In the end, President Madison led the U.S. to victory and put an end to England's threat of taking over the country. He retired after his second term ended.

The War of 1812 is also called America's second war of independence.

| 1809 | 1810 | 1811 | 1812 |
|---|---|---|---|
| James Madison takes office | The U.S. Census counts 7.2 million Americans | Venezuela declares its independence from Spain | The War of 1812 begins |

Democrat-Republican

The War of 1812 is also known as America's second war of independence with the British Empire. The war officially began with an American declaration. Why were the Americans upset? First, Britain introduced trade restrictions that impeded American trade with France. Secondly, Britain began forcing American citizens to serve in the Royal Navy. And finally, Britain began supporting American Indians who were attacking American settlers in what are now Ohio, Indiana, Illinois, Michigan, and Wisconsin.

The British struck a huge blow during the war by invading Washington, D.C., and burning the White House to the ground. The U.S. countered by successfully defending Baltimore and routing the English at the Battle of New Orleans. In the end, the United States won the war and Britain realized it would never regain control of its old colonies.

Did you know that the Battle of New Orleans took place <u>after</u> the war was over?

Due to poor means of communication, the commanders on both sides didn't receive news of the war's end until after the battle was fought!

Francis Scott Key penned the words to the American National Anthem during the War of 1812!

## PRESIDENT QUIZ

| WHO AM I? | TRIVIA |
| --- | --- |
| 1913 - 1921  | Who was elected president a record four times? |
| Page 60 | Page 68 |

"All men having power ought to be distrusted to a certain degree."
— James Madison

| 1813 | 1814 | 1815 | 1816 |
| --- | --- | --- | --- |
| James Madison begins his second term as war continues | Washington, D.C., is captured and burned by the British | America wins The War of 1812 | America's first savings bank opens |

# #5  James Monroe
## (1817 - 1825)

James Monroe was born in Virginia in 1758. As a student, he excelled in many subjects. When he was sixteen, he enrolled in the College of William and Mary, but the atmosphere leading to the Revolutionary War compelled Monroe to quit his studies and fight for America's freedom.

Born: April 28, 1758
Died: July 4, 1831

Shortly after the battles of Lexington and Concord in June of 1775, Monroe joined twenty-four men and raided an arsenal where they took muskets and swords. He later joined the Continental Army and served with distinction at the Battle of Trenton. After the war, he studied law under Thomas Jefferson and married Elizabeth Kortright. As time passed, he became a leading candidate for the presidency.

With the Federalist Party in disarray, James Monroe became president by winning the Elections of 1816 and 1820. In office, he began what is known as the "Monroe Doctrine" which stated that the U.S. would no longer tolerate European interference or colonization in both North and South America. The U.S. also purchased Florida from Spain for five million dollars which, in turn, prompted war between America and the Seminole Indians living there. President Monroe retired after his second term ended.

As this old political cartoon suggests, the U.S. didn't want European countries to interfere with North and South America.

| 1817 | 1818 | 1819 | 1820 |
|------|------|------|------|
| James Monroe takes office as new president | In Canada, the 49th Parallel is set between the U.S. and Britain | The U.S. and Spain set borders in the Southwest | The Missouri Compromise settles a slavery dispute in Congress |

The United States saw its borders with neighboring nations better defined while James Monroe was president. In the northwest, the U.S. and Britain established the 49th parallel as the border between Canada (controlled by Great Britain at the time) and the Louisiana Purchase Territory (controlled by the U.S.). In the south, the U.S. expanded its borders by purchasing Florida from Spain in 1819. The U.S. also received territory in what is now south-western Louisiana from the Spanish that same year.

The American Colonization Society (ACS) was established in Washington, D.C., in 1816 for the purpose of returning freed African-American slaves to Africa. It was founded by a small group of men, including Paul Cuffee who captained voyages to Sierra Leone where he helped some African-Americans establish a new colony.

In 1821, the society began transporting more freed African-Americans to other areas along Africa's west coast. With the help of the ACS, these new colonists pulled together, grew in power, and founded the Republic of Liberia. Without a doubt this new nation was unique to Africa. It modeled its government similar to that of the United States and even named its capital Monrovia, in honor of President James Monroe who supported Liberia's existence.

Chancy Brown, Sergeant at Arms of Liberian Senate

## PRESIDENT QUIZ

### WHO AM I?

1881 - 1881

Page 44

### TRIVIA

Which president was the hero of the Battle of New Orleans?

Page 18

"Our country may be likened to a new house. We lack many things, but we possess the most precious of all - liberty!"

— James Monroe

| 1820 | 1821 | 1822 | 1824 |
|---|---|---|---|
| The U.S. Census counts 9.6 million Americans | Mexico wins its independence from Spain | Florida becomes a U.S. territory | The country of Liberia is formed by freed American slaves |

Born: July 11, 1767
Died: February 23, 1848

John Quincy Adams was born in 1767 in Massachusetts. He was the son of John Adams, the second president of the United States. When John Quincy was young, he spent much of his time in France and the Netherlands with his father who was on diplomatic missions. During this time, he mastered the French and Dutch languages.

In 1797, John Quincy was appointed as Minister to Prussia. While in London, he married Louisa Johnson, the daughter of an American merchant. He returned to America and was elected to the Massachusetts State Senate; appointed as the first ever U.S Minister to Russia; and negotiated the Treaty of Ghent which ended the War of 1812. He was certainly a man on the move and he ran for president in 1824.

John Quincy Adams didn't receive the most popular votes or electoral votes in the Election of 1824, but he was elected by the House of Representatives to be the next president anyway! Many of his opponents were supporters of Andrew Jackson (who had the most popular and electoral votes) and they felt robbed. So, they did almost everything they could to keep President Adams from succeeding while he was in office. When the next election came around, President Adams was defeated by (you guessed it!) Andrew Jackson.

John Quincy Adams negotiated the Treaty of Ghent which ended the War of 1812.

| 1825 | 1825 | 1826 | 1827 |
|---|---|---|---|
| John Quincy Adams takes office | The Erie Canal is opened in New York | America's first railroad is chartered in Massachusetts | America's first African-American newspaper is founded |

The Election of 1824 was unique and featured four strong candidates for president. The initial electoral count had Andrew Jackson in the lead with 99 electoral votes; Adams was second with 84 votes; William Crawford had 41; and Henry Clay had 37. Now, because Andrew Jackson didn't carry more than 50% of the total electoral votes (he needed at least 131), it was left to the House of Representatives to determine who would be the next president. The House met to decide the matter, voted, and elected John Quincy Adams to be the next president. Andrew Jackson was understandably in shock with this outcome and America got a strange lesson in the presidential election process.

When the House of Representatives met to consider who would be the next president following the 1824 election, only the top three candidates could be considered. As a result, Henry Clay wasn't on the ballot. Still, Clay had a tremendous impact on the election's outcome because he was Speaker of the House of Representatives. From his position, Clay used his power of persuasion to steer voters away from Jackson (whom Clay didn't like) and to Adams, the eventual winner. William Crawford was also on the ballot, but he didn't pose a threat to either Adams or Jackson.

Noah Webster published his "An American Dictionary of the English Language" in 1828 and it was no easy task. He began work on the project in 1807 and learned a staggering twenty-six languages to bolster his etymology of words!

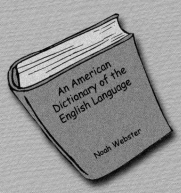

An American Dictionary of the English Language

Noah Webster

## PRESIDENT QUIZ

### WHO AM I?

1837 - 1841

Page 20

### TRIVIA

Who was president when abolitionist John Brown was hanged?

Page 34

"If your actions inspire others to dream more, learn more, do more and become more, you are a leader."

— John Quincy Adams

| 1827 | 1827 | 1828 | 1828 |
|---|---|---|---|
| New Orleans celebrates its first Mardi Gras | Ludwig von Beethoven dies in Europe | Noah Webster publishes his new dictionary | Simon Bolivar rises to power in South America |

# #7  Andrew Jackson
## (1829 - 1837)

Andrew Jackson was born in South Carolina in 1767. At the age of thirteen, he was imprisoned by the British during the Revolutionary War and nearly starved to death. One soldier even slashed Jackson with a sword when Jackson refused to shine the soldier's boots! Years after the war, Jackson became a lawyer and settled in Tennessee.

Before the turn of the century, Jackson became a U.S. Representative and then a U.S. Senator for Tennessee, but his actions in the War of 1812 threw him into the spotlight. After defeating Tecumseh and being promoted to Major General, he took charge of the American defenses at New Orleans and, with only 5,000 men, defeated 7,500 British troops. Andrew Jackson became a hero and decided to run for the presidency.

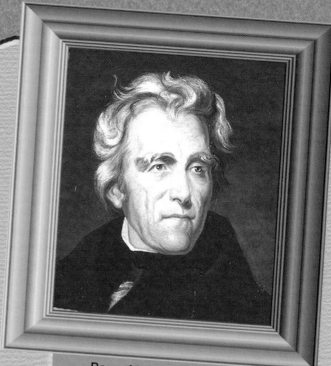

Born: March 15, 1767
Died: June 8, 1845

Andrew Jackson lost the Presidential Election of 1824 despite having the most popular votes, but he came back to win the Elections of 1828 and 1832. In office, President Jackson tried and failed to get Congress to abolish the Electoral College. He also removed many Indian tribes from their lands and forced them to move further west. After his second term ended, President Jackson retired to "The Hermitage", his Tennessee estate.

Andrew Jackson was slashed by a British soldier when he was a child.

| 1829 | 1830 | 1830 | 1831 |
|---|---|---|---|
| Andrew Jackson takes office | The Mormon church is organized in New York | The U.S. Census counts 12.8 million Americans | Nat Turner leads a slave uprising in Virginia and fails |

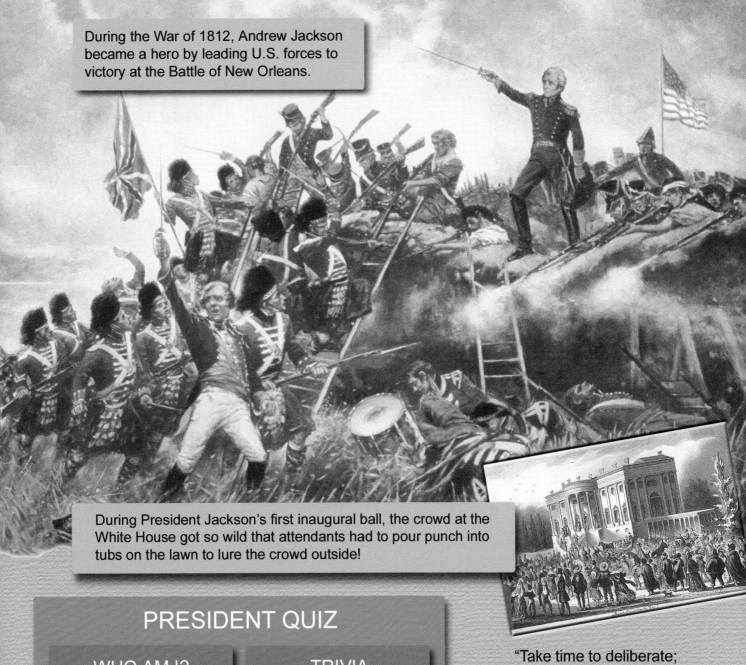

During the War of 1812, Andrew Jackson became a hero by leading U.S. forces to victory at the Battle of New Orleans.

During President Jackson's first inaugural ball, the crowd at the White House got so wild that attendants had to pour punch into tubs on the lawn to lure the crowd outside!

## PRESIDENT QUIZ

### WHO AM I?

1945 - 1953

Page 70

### TRIVIA

Which president was dumped by his own party in 1856?

Page 32

"Take time to deliberate; but when the time for action arrives, stop thinking and go in."
— Andrew Jackson

| 1832 | 1834 | 1835 | 1837 |
|------|------|------|------|
| The U.S. intensifies its war against American Indians | Congress creates Oklahoma as an Indian territory | Slaves from Florida revolt and join the Seminole Indians | The U.S. recognizes the Republic of Texas as a country |

# #8 Martin Van Buren
## (1837 - 1841)

Martin Van Buren was born in 1782 in New York. Because all previous presidents were born prior to 1776, he was the first one to be "born" an American citizen. He began studying law at the young age of fourteen and became a lawyer when he was twenty. In 1807, he married Hannah Hoes, his childhood sweetheart.

Born: December 5, 1782
Died: July 24, 1862

Van Buren's wealth grew with his law practice and he soon became active in politics. He was elected a U.S. Senator from New York in 1821 and, a few years later, became the state's governor. But his stint as governor didn't last long. Two months after taking office, he accepted President Jackson's offer to become Secretary of State. Then, during Jackson's second term, Van Buren became President Jackson's vice president.

After Texas won its independence from Mexico, it applied for statehood and President Van Buren blocked the move. As a result, Texas would have to wait.

Martin Van Buren became president after winning the Election of 1836. Upon taking office, he maintained nearly all of President Jackson's cabinet members. During his term, he angered many when he denied Texas its request to join the United States. He also was blamed for the economic turmoil stemming from the Panic of 1837 and a commercial crisis which began a year later. Because of these troubled times, he was labeled Martin Van "Ruin" and failed in his re-election attempt.

| 1837 | 1837 | 1838 | 1838 |
|---|---|---|---|
| Martin Van Buren takes office | The Panic of 1837 leads to bank runs and food riots | Samuel Morse demonstrates the telegraph | Frederick Douglas escapes from slavery |

The inhabitants of Texas (many of whom were American settlers) won their independence from Mexico in 1836 and tried to join the United States a year later. President Van Buren blocked this from happening, partly because he wanted America to stay at peace with Mexico. As a result, Texas stood alone as its own country for a while. That's right, it's own country!

_____

After losing the Election of 1840 and being turned down by the Democratic Party in 1844, Van Buren came back and ran for president in 1848 as the Free Soil Party's candidate!

He didn't do too well.

He received no electoral votes and barely 10% of the popular vote.

When slaves took over the Cuban ship "Amistad" and ended up in the United States, President Van Buren sided with the Spanish Government that wanted all the slaves returned to its custody as runaways. However, the Supreme Court had the final say in the matter and allowed the slaves to freely return to Africa. After the Supreme Court's decision, the freed Africans set sail for home.

## PRESIDENT QUIZ

### WHO AM I?

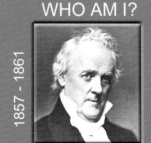

1857 - 1861

Page 34

### TRIVIA

Who was the president during the Mexican-American War?

Page 26

"The government should not be guided by temporary excitement, but by sober second thought."

— Martin Van Buren

| 1839 | 1839 | 1840 | 1840 |
|------|------|------|------|
| Dueling is outlawed in Washington, D.C. | The Liberty Party forms in opposition to slavery | America's first college of dental surgery opens in Baltimore | The U.S. Census counts 17.1 million Americans |

# #9 William H. Harrison
## (1841 - 1841)

William Henry Harrison was born in 1773 in Virginia. He was the youngest of seven children and the last president to be born a British subject. Harrison joined the U.S. Army when he was eighteen and fought Indians at the Battle of Fallen Timbers in 1794. He married Anna Symmes and the two had ten children together.

Harrison resigned from the military in 1797 and was appointed Secretary of the Northwest Territory. In the following years, he fought for the rights of many settlers in the area and became the first governor of the Indiana Territory. Strangely enough, while holding this political position, Harrison led U.S. troops to defeat Indians at the battle of Tippecanoe. This victory made Harrison a popular man.

Born: February 9, 1773
Died: April 4, 1841

Riding his popularity, Harrison won the Presidential Election of 1840 and took the oath of office on March 4, 1841. On that cold and rainy day, he stood outside and delivered the longest inaugural address in U.S. history. He then rode in a parade. Sadly, President Harrison developed a cold on March 26th and died from its complications a few weeks later. In the end, President Harrison was the first president to die in office and a question was raised as to whether the vice president could indeed become the next president! The answer was yes, he can.

William Henry Harrison fought at the Battle of Fallen Timbers when he was only eighteen years old. He later led U.S. forces to victory at the Battle of Tippecanoe.

| 1841 | 1841 | 1841 | 1841 |
|------|------|------|------|
| William H. Harrison takes office | President Harrison delivers the longest inaugural address | President Harrison receives many White House visitors | President Harrison refuses to dismiss many Democrat appointees |

While William Henry Harrison was governor of the Indiana Territory, white settlers were encroaching upon Indian lands illegally. To counter this, Shawnee chieftain Tecumseh launched a movement among the Shawnees and other local tribes that attempted to unite the Indians and prevent further expansion of white settlers into their territories. His confederation of tribes built a settlement where the Wabash and Tippecanoe rivers met and this settlement became a focal point of Tecumseh's movement. On November 7, 1811, Harrison took 1,100 men to this settlement and battled the Shawnees (minus Tecumseh who was away recruiting). Though the actual battle was considered a draw by most historians, its aftermath favored Harrison. Many Shawnees lost the desire to remain united and Harrison was seen as a hero.

Did you know that someone can't catch a "cold" by just standing in the rain or cold?

The illness can only be contracted by coming into contact with someone who is carrying the virus. So, contrary to what you may have heard, President Harrison's standing in the cold rain didn't cause him to die.

President Harrison on his deathbed.

Harrison's 32 days in office marked the shortest tenure of all the presidents.

## PRESIDENT QUIZ

### WHO AM I?

1849 - 1850

Page 28

### TRIVIA

Which president sent Commodore Perry to Japan?

Page 30

"Sir, I wish to understand the true principles of the Government. I wish them carried out. I ask nothing more."

— William H. Harrison

| 1841 | 1841 | 1841 | 1841 |
|---|---|---|---|
| President Harrison becomes ill with a "cold" | Cornstarch is patented | President Harrison develops pneumonia | President Harrison dies |

# John Tyler
## (1841 - 1845)

John Tyler was born in Virginia in 1790 and received a quality education. At the age of twelve, he entered a prep school. He entered college three years later and graduated when he was only seventeen years old. By the age of twenty, Tyler was a lawyer! When the War of 1812 began, he joined a militia to fight against the British.

Born: March 29, 1790
Died: January 18, 1862

John Tyler served in the militia during the War of 1812.

After the war, Tyler began his political career at the state level in Virginia. He became a U.S. Representative in 1816 and a U.S. Senator in 1827. In 1836, he ran as a vice-presidential candidate for the Whig party, but the ticket came in third place in the general election. Four years later, in 1840, he once again became his party's choice for vice president with William Henry Harrison heading the ticket. Together, Harrison and Tyler won the election and John Tyler became America's new vice president.

John Tyler became president following the death of President Harrison in 1841. During his term, he upset members of his party (the Whigs) by practically vetoing every bill that crossed his desk. In fact, after having vetoed one bill, the Whigs changed its wording to meet President Tyler's approval and he vetoed it again! The Whigs were enraged and, as a result, expelled President Tyler from their party. When it came time for the next election, the Whigs chose Henry Clay as its nominee and President Tyler didn't run. Instead, he threw his support to James K. Polk, a Democrat.

John Tyler became the first president to not be elected to the position.

| 1841 | 1841 | 1841 | 1842 |
|---|---|---|---|
| John Tyler becomes president after Harrision dies | Wagon trains begin leaving Missouri for California | The "Amistad" survivors return to Africa to be free | The sewing machine is patented |

Several years before John Tyler became president, the American economy was so bad that many Americans either lost their jobs or saw their wages cut by as much as 50%. People were suffering and looking for a better life. One small group of seventy people believed they would find prosperity in the west, so they departed Missouri in wagons in 1841. Not long afterwards, more and more Americans followed this group's lead and traveled in wagon trains to the Oregon and California territories. Many of them were led by promises of rich soil and paradise. Sadly, what most found when they reached their destinations was anything but. The land was untamed; supplies were scarce; and the threat of being robbed or killed was high.

The Oregon Trail, the Santa Fe Trail, and the Mormon Trail were a few of the routes wagon trains used to go west.

It's believed that nearly 400,000 Americans traveled along these trails between 1841 and 1866.

The first electric telegraph message was sent on May 1, 1844.

It said that Henry Clay was the Whig Party's nominee for president.

## PRESIDENT QUIZ

### WHO AM I?

1850 - 1853

Page 30

### TRIVIA

"Old Rough and Ready" was this president's nickname

Page 28

"Wealth can only be accumulated by the earnings of industry and the savings of frugality."
— John Tyler

| 1843 | 1844 | 1844 | 1845 |
|---|---|---|---|
| The typewriter is patented | The first telegraph line is completed | Goodyear patents vulcanization of rubber | Edgar Allen Poe's "Raven" is published |

# James K. Polk
## (1845 - 1849)

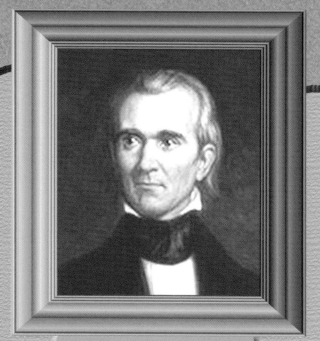

James K. Polk was born in North Carolina in 1795. In 1806, he moved with his family to Tennessee. Polk suffered from poor health and had to have an operation to remove urinary stones when he was sixteen years old. This surgery took place in Kentucky with brandy used for anesthetic.

Born: November 2, 1795
Died: June 15, 1849

While attending the University of North Carolina, Polk took part in debates and learned the art of oratory. After graduating, he studied law in Nashville, became popular, and began his political career. Polk was elected to the Tennessee state legislature in 1823; became a U.S. Representative in 1825; and served as Tennessee's governor from 1839 to 1841. In 1844, he ran for president.

James K. Polk won the Election of 1844 and promised to only serve one term. In office, he annexed Texas into the Union, knowing that this would anger Mexico. He also expanded U.S. boundaries by acquiring the Oregon Territory through negotiations with Great Britain and territories in the southwest after having a "small" war with Mexico. True to his word, after his term drew to a close, he didn't pursue being re-elected. He went into retirement after leaving office.

The U.S. defeated Mexico in the Mexican-American War while James K. Polk was president.

| 1845 | 1846 | 1846 | 1847 |
|------|------|------|------|
| James K. Polk takes office | The Mexican-American War begins after Texas becomes a state | Mormons travel west from Missouri to Utah | The U.S. Marines capture Mexico City |

Democrat

The Mexican-American War lasted from 1846 to 1848 and was the result of the U.S. admitting Texas to the Union as a state. During the war, American forces seized large parts of northern Mexico, blockaded the Mexican coast, and invaded Mexico City. After its capital was captured, the Mexican government was left with few options and was ready to make peace on U.S. terms. The Treaty of Guadalupe Hidalgo was signed by both sides and the war ended. As part of this treaty, Mexico gave up its claim to Texas and sold what are now the American states of California, Nevada, Utah, and Arizona.

Many Americans who fought during the Mexican-American War became famous in the coming years. Zachary Taylor was a general and became President of the United States. Winfield Scott was also a general and grew to legendary status as both a military strategist and commander. Ulysses S. Grant, George B. McClellan, Ambrose Burnside, Robert E. Lee, James Longstreet, "Stonewall" Jackson, and George Meade served as junior officers in Mexico and became household names as military leaders during the Civil War. And Jefferson Davis became the President of the Confederacy during the Civil War.

On the other side of the conflict, Mexico's General Santa Anna succeeded in becoming his country's president in 1853. He was later forced from office, declared a traitor, and lived in various parts of the world including Cuba and the United States. He was allowed to return to Mexico in 1874 and died two years later.

General Santa Anna

## PRESIDENT QUIZ

### WHO AM I?

1853 - 1857

Page 32

### TRIVIA

Who beat Samuel Tilden in the Election of 1876?

Page 42

"One great object of the Constitution was to restrain majorities from oppressing minorities or encroaching upon their just rights."
— James K. Polk

| 1848 | 1848 | 1848 | 1849 |
|------|------|------|------|
| Chinese immigrants begin arriving in San Francisco | The Mexican-American War comes to an end | Gas lights are installed in the White House | Elizabeth Blackwell becomes America's first female doctor |

# #12 Zachary Taylor
## (1849 - 1850)

Zachary Taylor was born in 1784 in Virginia. He spent much of his youth in the Kentucky frontier and received tutoring whenever his father could find someone able. In 1808, Taylor joined the army. He fought in the Indiana Territory during the War of 1812 and against the Seminole Indians in Florida. Later, he went to Texas after it became a state.

In Texas, Taylor fought against Mexico during the Mexican-American War and became a hero after winning several battles where he was outnumbered. After the war, in 1848, he became the Whig Party's candidate for president despite him being a southern slave owner at a time when many southern states were ready to secede from the Union.

Born: November 24, 1784
Died: July 9, 1850

Zachary Taylor won the Election of 1848. When he took office as the nation's twelfth president, the question of whether or not slavery should be allowed in the new Western Territories was a hot topic. Despite being a slave owner himself, he angered many southerners when he urged anti-slave territories in what are now Utah, New Mexico, and California to seek statehood quickly. Sadly, on July 9, 1850, President Taylor contracted an unknown illness and died. He was later buried near his parents' graves in Kentucky.

After gold is discovered in California, many Americans begin moving to the West, looking for riches.

| 1849 | 1849 | 1849 | 1849 |
|------|------|------|------|
| Zachary Taylor takes office | Abraham Lincoln gets his first patent | A gas mask is patented | Gold is discovered in California |

Zachary Taylor had an interesting family that clearly illustrates the divisions that the future Civil War would bring to many Americans. His son, Richard served as a Confederate Lieutenant General during the Civil War and his daughter, Sarah, married future Confederate President Jefferson Davis in 1835. Sarah died of malaria three months after her marriage. In contrast to Richard, President Taylor's brother, Joseph Pannill Taylor, served as a Brigadier General in the Union Army during the Civil War.

It is believed President Taylor died of acute gastroenteritis after he consumed large amounts of cherries and milk during July 4th festivities held in Washington, D.C. After becoming ill, his doctors treated him with calomel, opium, and various other "healing" drugs of the time. He was also bled and blistered. In hindsight, these acts to save the president's life most likely contributed to President Taylor's untimely death.

Zachary Taylor in command at the Battle of Buena Vista in 1847.

Zachary Taylor was known as "Old Rough and Ready" and served in the U.S. Army for forty years prior to becoming president. During his lengthy military career, he fought in the War of 1812, the Black Hawk War, and the Second Seminole War. He also fought in the Mexican-American War where he became popular to many Americans.

## PRESIDENT QUIZ

### WHO AM I?

1897 - 1901

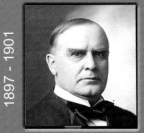

Page 54

### TRIVIA

Who owned a newspaper in Ohio before becoming president?

Page 62

"I have always done my duty. I am ready to die. My only regret is for the friends I leave behind me."

— Zachary Taylor

| 1850 | 1850 | 1850 | 1850 |
|---|---|---|---|
| The city of San Francisco is incorporated | The U.S. Census counts 23.1 million Americans | America's first female medical school opens | President Taylor dies |

# #13  Millard Fillmore
## (1850 - 1853)

Millard Fillmore was born in what was called the "frontier" of New York in 1800. He was born a few weeks after George Washington's death. Fillmore had a tough time obtaining an education due to the area's poor conditions, but when he was nineteen, he landed a job working for a judge and began studying law.

In the following years, Fillmore became a lawyer; married Abigail Powers; had two children; and entered politics. He held a state assembly position and later became a U.S. Representative. In 1848, members of his party wanted a vice presidential candidate who could help them win the election. They chose Fillmore and the strategy worked. Zachary Taylor was elected president and Milliard Fillmore became the vice president.

Born:  January 7, 1800
Died:  March 8, 1874

Millard Fillmore became president following President Zachary Taylor's death. In office, President Fillmore replaced members of the cabinet and tried to calm the slavery debate between northern and southern states. Many members of his political party (the Whigs) became very upset with Fillmore's policies, so they dropped President Fillmore and chose General Winfield Scott to represent them in the next election. Scott lost the 1852 Presidential Election and the Whig Party began to fall apart.

San Francisco is devastated by fire on May 4th, 1850.

| 1850 | 1850 | 1850 | 1851 |
|---|---|---|---|
| Millard Fillmore takes office | The Great San Francisco Fire erupts in California | Slave trade is no longer allowed in Washington, D.C. | Isaac Singer patents the sewing machine |

President Fillmore promoted American trade by sending Commodore Perry to Japan. When it opened its ports, Japan quickly developed into a modernized nation.

The Fugitive Slave Law of 1850 led some abolitionists to create posters to warn African-Americans to watch out! Another abolitionist, Harriet Beecher Stowe, told of slavery's horrors in her book "Uncle Tom's Cabin."

CAUTIO
COLORED PEOP
OF BOSTON, ONE & A
You are hereby respectfully CAUTIONE
advised, to avoid conversing with th
Watchmen and Police Offi
of Boston,
For since the recent ORDER OF THE MAY
ALDERMEN, they are empowered to act a
KIDNAPPERS
AND
Slave Catcher
And they have already been actually employed
KIDNAPPING, CATCHING, AND KEEPI
SLAVES. Therefore, if you value your LIBERT
and the *Welfare of the Fugitives* among you, Sh
them in every possible manner, as so many *HOUN*
on the track of the most unfortunate of your race.
Keep a Sharp Look Out fo
KIDNAPPERS, and hav
TOP EYE open.
APRIL 24, 1851.

## PRESIDENT QUIZ

### WHO AM I?

1889 - 1893

Page 50

### TRIVIA

Who became president after William Henry Harrison died?

Page 24

"May God save the country, for it is evident that the people will not."

— Millard Fillmore

CALIFORNIA
STATEHOOD
1850

| 1851 | 1851 | 1852 | 1852 |
|---|---|---|---|
| The telescope is patented by Alvan Clark | Herman Melville's "Moby Dick" is published | Harriet Beecher Stowe's "Uncle Tom's Cabin" is published | Ohio enacts child labor laws to protect children |

# #14 Franklin Pierce
## (1853 - 1857)

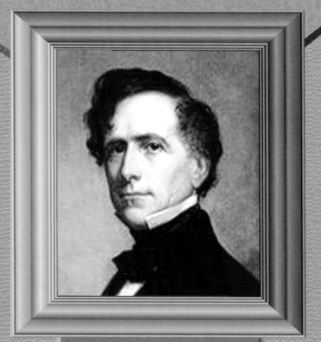

Franklin Pierce was born in a log cabin in New Hampshire in 1804. His family was poor but Pierce was able to go to college where he graduated third in his class. He then completed law school and opened a practice in 1827. Several years later, he married Jane Appleton. They had three children. Sadly, all three died in childhood.

Born: November 23, 1804
Died: October 8, 1869

Pierce entered politics at the young age of twenty-four and held several positions in New Hampshire. When the Mexican-American War started in 1846, he postponed his political career and volunteered to fight. This decision nearly cost him his life. At the Battle of Contreras, Pierce seriously wounded his leg. After it healed, he returned to New Hampshire to continue his political career and, in 1852, he decided to run for president.

Franklin Pierce was seriously wounded at the Battle of Contreras during the Mexican-American War.

Franklin Pierce became president by winning the Election of 1852. Before he took office, the debate over slavery was still a minor issue; however, shortly into his term, the passage of the Kansas-Nebraska Act (which repealed the Missouri Compromise) brought the question of slavery in the West to the forefront of national politics. To the public, President Pierce was perceived as a man who supported slavery and, because of this, he did not receive his party's nomination in the next election. President Pierce left office in 1857.

| 1853 | 1853 | 1853 | 1854 |
|---|---|---|---|
| Franklin Pierce takes office | Harriet Tubman starts the "Underground Railroad" | The Gadsden Purchase is made with Mexico | The first meeting of the Republican Party takes place |

Southerners feared they would soon be outnumbered in Congress and would no longer be able to keep African-Americans in slavery. The passage of the Kansas-Nebraska Act in 1854 helped pacify these fears by allowing the peoples of territories in the West to decide if slavery would be allowed within their borders. A short time later, areas such as Kansas became hotbeds of violence when abolitionists clashed with those who wanted slavery.

In the 1856 Presidential Election, the Democratic Party dumped President Franklin Pierce, choosing instead to back James Buchanan for president.

Four years later, the Democrats dumped Buchanan and extended their hands once again to Pierce. Pierce turned them down, thus paving the way for Abraham Lincoln to win.

Harriet Tubman escaped slavery in 1849 and, during Pierce's presidency, began a network called the "Underground Railroad" that helped other slaves escape. Aided by abolitionists who worked with her, Tubman helped thousands of runaway slaves reach Canada, Mexico, and Northern states where they could be free.

Harriet Tubman became a hero and died in 1913 at the age of ninety-three.

## PRESIDENT QUIZ

### WHO AM I?

1877 - 1881

Page 42

### TRIVIA

Which president was a Lieutenant General during the Civil War?

Page 40

"The storm of frenzy and faction must inevitably dash itself in vain against the unshaken rock of the Constitution."

— Franklin Pierce

| 1854 | 1855 | 1856 | 1857 |
|---|---|---|---|
| Abraham Lincoln makes his first political speech | American William Walker conquers Nicaragua | Violence erupts in Kansas over the issue of slavery | The Supreme Court rules that slaves can't be U.S. citizens |

# James Buchanan
## (1857 - 1861)

Born: April 23, 1791
Died: June 1, 1868

James Buchanan was born in 1791 in Pennsylvania. In college, he was expelled for poor behavior. He asked for a second chance and went on to graduate with honors. Afterwards, he became a lawyer and fought in the War of 1812 where he helped defend Baltimore from the British. After the war, he turned his sights to a career in politics.

Buchanan became a U.S. Representative in 1821 and was re-elected several times. Afterwards, he wore many hats. He was the Minister to Russia under President Jackson; the Secretary of State under President Polk; and the Minister to the Court of St. James under President Pierce. When the 1856 Presidential Election came around, he was the Democratic Party's top pick for the presidency.

James Buchanan won the Election of 1856 amid boiling tensions between Northern and Southern states over the issue of slavery. In office, he did little to cool these flames and more and more people were ready to fight. When the next election came, the Democratic Party had a schism (between North and South, of course) and the Republicans won. During President Buchanan's final days in the White House, he did little while the Southern states seceded from the Union, leaving Abraham Lincoln and the nation with a crisis.

Abolitionist John Brown and his men were captured after raiding the federal arsenal at Harper's Ferry, Virginia, in 1858. His attempt to start a slave revolt demonstrated that many were willing to fight to end slavery.

| 1857 | 1857 | 1858 | 1858 |
|------|------|------|------|
| James Buchanan takes office | The first U.S. elevator is installed (in New York) | John Brown raids the arsenal at Harper's Ferry, Virginia | The Trans-Atlantic Telegraph Cable is completed |

John Brown was an abolitionist who increased tensions between Northern and Southern states during President Buchanan's term of office. After leading the Pottawatomie Massacre in Kansas in 1856, Brown returned East, raised some money, and made plans to raid the U.S. Arsenal at Harper's Ferry, Virginia. With barely twenty men, he hoped to secure the arsenal, seize weapons, and lead a slave revolt. His plan was launched on October 16, 1859, when he captured the arsenal, took hostages, and cut telegraph wires. However, the town's people fought back and blocked Brown's escape route. Trapped for two days, Brown and his men were soon overwhelmed by U.S. Marines that President Buchanan dispatched and were captured. After a swift trial, Brown was found guilty and hanged for treason against the Commonwealth of Virginia. His death soon became a rallying cry for many opposed to slavery and an omen of more deaths to come.

John Brown walks to the scaffold to be hanged.

In April of 1860, the Pony Express began making mail runs from Missouri to California. At that time, the most direct and fastest means of communication to the West was horseback. Conditions for the riders were harsh and many died when they encountered bad weather and hostile Indians along the 2,000-mile route.

## PRESIDENT QUIZ

### WHO AM I?

1865 - 1869

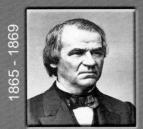

Page 38

### TRIVIA

Which president was born in Arkansas?

Page 88

"What is right and what is practical are two different things."

— James Buchanan

| 1859 | 1859 | 1860 | 1860 |
|---|---|---|---|
| The first successful oil well is drilled (in Pennsylvania) | Charles Darwin publishes "On the Origin of Species" | The U.S. Census counts 31.4 million Americans | The Pony Express begins delivering mail |

# #16 Abraham Lincoln
## (1861 - 1865)

Abraham Lincoln was born in a one-room log cabin in Kentucky in 1809. When he was seven years old, he moved with his family to Indiana. His mother died two years later. In 1830, his family moved to Illinois. Lincoln went to school for about eighteen months in his youth, but he loved to read and, simply put, educated himself!

Despite lacking a formal education, Lincoln became a lawyer and, in 1846, a U.S. Representative for the Whig party. He served one term in Congress and then resumed his law practice. In 1856, Lincoln helped organize a new political party, the Republican Party. Four years later, in 1860, he became its candidate for president. The self-educated Lincoln was ready for the White House.

Born: February 12, 1809
Died: April 15, 1865

Abraham Lincoln won the Presidential Election of 1860 and was re-elected in 1864. While in office, he was faced with the greatest crisis in American history, the Civil War. During his tenure, President Lincoln led the cause to preserve the Union; emancipated slaves in the southern states; and witnessed hundreds of thousands of soldiers dying on both sides. In the end, President Lincoln helped win the war and the admiration of many people. However, while he was watching a play in Ford's Theater in Washington, D.C., he was killed by an assassin's bullet. The nation was left to mourn yet another great loss.

Abraham Lincoln's Union forces lost the First Battle of Bull Run, one of the earliest battles of the war.

As the Civil War progressed, the Union forces grew stronger and the tide of the war turned.

| 1861 | 1861 | 1861 | 1862 |
|---|---|---|---|
| Abraham Lincoln takes office | The Civil War begins with the seige of Fort Sumter | To finance the war, the U.S. levies its first income tax | America introduces "paper" currency for the first time |

Republican (1860) / National Union (1864)

No doubt, the Civil War was the most trying event of President Lincoln's administration and the nation. In fact, when Lincoln was sworn into office on March 3, 1861, the Confederacy (consisting of seven southern states) was already established, having elected Jefferson Davis as its president. Several other states joined the Confederacy in the coming months and a devastating war ensued that lasted for four years. In the early stages of the war, the Confederate forces looked as if they might prevail in preserving the Confederacy. However, after numerous battles, the Union Army was able to force the Confederacy to surrender. The cost of the war was high and not just in dollars. The Union lost nearly 360,000 men to battle and disease and the Confederacy lost roughly 260,000. The greatest benefit from the war was that slavery in the United States was ended.

John Wilkes Booth shot President Lincoln in Ford's Theater in Washington, D.C., while the president was watching a play. Booth, an actor and a supporter of the Confederacy, ran from the scene but was later killed when Union forces tracked him to a farmhouse in Virginia. President Lincoln died shortly after the shooting.

Abraham Lincoln is regarded as one of America's greatest presidents. His name and image appear in many places, including the five-dollar bill and penny.

## PRESIDENT QUIZ

### WHO AM I?

1797 - 1801

Page 8

### TRIVIA

Who defeated John Adams in 1801 to become president?

Page 10

"How many legs does a dog have if you call the tail a leg? Four, calling the tail a leg doesn't make it a leg."
— Abraham Lincoln

| 1863 | 1863 | 1865 | 1865 |
|------|------|------|------|
| The fire extinguisher is patented | Union forces win the Battle of Gettysburg | Confederate General Robert E. Lee surrenders | President Lincoln is assassinated at Ford's Theater |

# #17 Andrew Johnson
## (1865 - 1869)

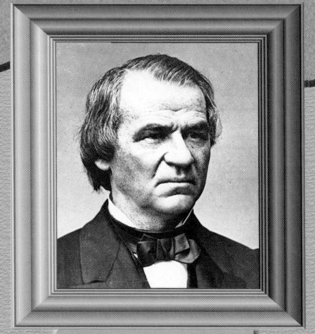

Andrew Johnson was born in North Carolina in 1808. In his youth, he worked as a tailor and taught himself to read and write. He later moved to Tennessee and married Eliza McCradle. Johnson entered politics by becoming mayor of Greeneville and, later, a U.S. Representative.

Born: December 29, 1808
Died: July 31, 1875

Johnson became Tennessee's governor in 1853. Four years later, he was elected to the U.S. Senate. When the Civil War started, his state joined the Confederacy but Johnson remained loyal to the Union. Because of this, he was thought to be the ideal candidate to run with Abraham Lincoln in 1864. The strategy worked. Lincoln won his re-election bid and Andrew Johnson became vice president.

Andrew Johnson became president after Lincoln's assassination and his primary task in office was dealing with the Reconstruction of the southern states that rebelled during the Civil War. He appointed leaders to govern the southern states and ran into trouble when they began passing Black Codes that limited the freedoms of African-Americans. When the Election of 1868 took place, President Johnson was so unpopular that he didn't get his party's endorsement. As a result, he dropped out of the race.

President Johnson was impeached in 1868 for removing Edwin Stanton as Secretary of War. He was charged with violating the Tenure of Office Act; tried before the U.S. Senate; and narrowly avoided a conviction.

| 1865 | 1865 | 1866 | 1866 |
|------|------|------|------|
| Andrew Johnson takes office | Slavery is abolished in the U.S. | The Civil War is formally declared over | Jesse James begins his robbery spree |

President Johnson upset many Republicans shortly after becoming president for a number of reasons. First, Johnson's policies toward the South were viewed as conciliatory in nature and, secondly, Johnson vetoed several civil rights bills that Republicans favored. For these reasons, a block of Republicans in the House of Representatives wanted the president removed from office. So, when they thought they had a chance, they impeached President Johnson, charging him for violating the Tenure of Office Act. The president was then tried before the Senate and found not guilty by one vote. If Johnson would have been found guilty, he would have been removed from office.

The Thirteenth Amendment to the Constitution abolished slavery and involuntary servitude (except as a punishment for a crime). It became the law of the land on December 6, 1865. Before becoming law, however, it was necessary for at least 75% of the 36 states existing at that time to approve the measure. So, when Georgia became the 27th state to give its approval, the amendment took effect nationwide. Slavery was officially abolished!

Though it was of no consequence, the nine "holdout" states did ratify the Thirteenth Amendment over time. Oregon, California, and Florida did so before the end of December 1865, and Iowa and New Jersey, the following year. Texas ratified the amendment in 1870 and Delaware waited until 1901. Remarkably, Kentucky didn't ratify the Thirteenth Amendment until 1976 and Mississippi, the last of the Civil War Era states, waited until 1995!

## PRESIDENT QUIZ

### WHO AM I?

1885 - 1889
1893 - 1897

Page 48

### TRIVIA

Which president was the son of President John Adams?

Page 16

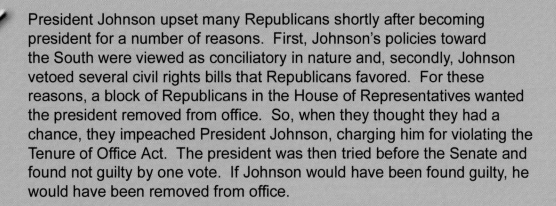

Jefferson Davis was indicted for treason in 1866, but the charge was later dropped.

"The goal to strive for is a poor government but a rich people."

— Andrew Johnson

| 1867 | 1867 | 1868 | 1869 |
|---|---|---|---|
| The U.S. purchases Alaska from Russia | Karl Marx publishes "Das Kapital" | Many Southern states re-enter the Union | Prosecutors drop treason case against Jefferson Davis |

# Ulysses S. Grant
## (1869 - 1877)

Ulysses S. Grant was born in 1822 in Ohio. When he was seventeen, he entered the U.S. Military Academy at West Point and developed a reputation as a fearless horseman. After graduating, Grant served under General Zachary Taylor during the Mexican-American War where he learned a lot about warfare.

After retiring from the military in 1854, Grant struggled as a farmer and a businessman. When the Civil War began, he was appointed to train volunteers in Illinois and quickly rose through the ranks as he proved successful on the battlefield. In 1864, he achieved the rank of Lieutenant General, a rank that had only previously been awarded to George Washington and Winfield Scott. In this position, he led the Union to victory over the Confederacy. After the war, he became a leading candidate for the presidency and he chose to run for office.

Born: April 27, 1822
Died: July 23, 1885

Ulysses S. Grant became president when he won the Elections of 1868 and 1872. In office, he devoted his time to the issue of Reconstruction. He also suppressed the Ku Klux Klan and saw passage of the 15th Amendment that gave freedmen the right to vote. However, Northerners were unhappy with an economic depression, and white Southerners were fighting to deny African-Americans their civil rights. These problems (and a few scandals) prevented President Grant from being elected to a third term.

Ulysses S. Grant led Union forces to victory on the battlefield during the Civil War.

| 1869 | 1869 | 1870 | 1871 |
|---|---|---|---|
| Ulysses S. Grant takes office | America's first professional baseball team is formed | The U.S. Census counts 39.8 million Americans | America repeals the federal income tax |

In 1873, the *Virginius* incident nearly thrust the U.S. into a war with Spain. The incident began when the U.S. merchant ship *Virginius* was taken captive by a Spanish warship for illegally carrying war materials and men to insurgents in Cuba (which happened to be owned by Spain at the time). Fifty-three of the passengers and crew of the *Virginius* were executed and many Americans called for war with Spain. However, after Spain's president apologized for the tragedy and paid a cash settlement to the families of the executed Americans, war was avoided. The U.S. Government did not authorize the shipment of war materials.

The Cincinnati Red Stockings hit the fields in 1869 as America's first professional baseball team. The Red Stockings defeated all its opponents, finishing the season with a 57-0 record.

Alexander Graham Bell patented the telephone in 1876. Ironically, he believed the invention to be an intrusion on his scientific work and refused to have one in his study.

## PRESIDENT QUIZ

### WHO AM I?

1974 - 1977

Page 80

### TRIVIA

Who became president after John F. Kennedy was assassinated?

Page 76

"Although a soldier by profession, I have never felt any sort of fondness for war, and I have never advocated it, except as a means of peace."

— Ulysses S. Grant

COLORADO STATEHOOD 1876

| 1873 | 1874 | 1875 | 1876 |
|---|---|---|---|
| P.T. Barnum's "Greatest Show on Earth" opens | "Boss" Tweed is convicted of fraud | Aristides wins the first Kentucky Derby (horse race) | Alexander Graham Bell patents the telephone |

Born: October 4, 1822
Died: January 17, 1893

Rutherford B. Hayes was born in Ohio in 1822. His father died shortly before his birth and an uncle acted as guardian. Hayes received a quality education and graduated from Harvard Law School in 1845. He began practicing law in his home state and, in 1852, married Lucy Webb. When the Civil War began, he quickly joined the Union forces.

During the war, Hayes rose to the rank of Brigadier General and became popular. After the war, he became a U.S. Representative and, a few years later, Ohio's governor. Then, with the 1876 Presidential Election approaching, he found himself the Republican nominee for president. However, because of scandals in the Grant administration (yes, Grant was a Republican too), the old commander was facing another tough battle that many thought he would lose.

Rutherford B. Hayes was a Brigadier General during the Civil War.

When the ballots were counted in the 1876 Presidential Election, Democrat Samuel Tilden received nearly 250,000 more votes than Rutherford B. Hayes, but Hayes became president anyway! How so? Because Hayes won the most electoral votes!

In office, President Hayes withdrew federal troops from Reconstructive states. Sadly, this left the door wide open in the South for segregation to enter and civil rights to exit. When it came time for the next election, President Hayes decided not to run.

| 1877 | 1878 | 1878 | 1879 |
|------|------|------|------|
| Rutherford B. Hayes takes office | Thomas Edison invents the phonograph | Electricity is furnished to some homes | Thomas Edison perfects the light bulb |

COLORED WAITING ROOM

PRIVATE PROPERTY NO PARKING
Driving through or Turning Around

Jim Crow Laws spread through the South when President Hayes was in office and, as this picture from the 1940s shows, had lasting effects.

Thomas Edison made a name for himself as an inventor when President Hayes was in office. Here he is with an early version of his phonograph.

## PRESIDENT QUIZ

### WHO AM I?

1881 - 1885

Page 46

### TRIVIA

Who was president when the Oklahoma Land Rush began?

Page 50

"The President of the United States should strive to be always mindful of the fact that he serves his party best who serves his country best."

— Rutherford B. Hayes

**1880**
France begins work on the Panama Canal in Central America

**1880**
The U.S. Census counts 50.1 million Americans

**1880**
Cha-ching, the first cash register is patented

**1881**
Kansas outlaws all alcoholic beverage sales in its state

# #20  James A. Garfield
## (1881 - 1881)

James A. Garfield was born in a log cabin in Ohio in 1831. He was raised in what was then known as "The Wilderness". In 1854, he graduated from Williams College with the highest honors in his class and went on to become a college president, a state senator, and a major general in the U.S. army.

Born: November 19, 1831
Died: September 19, 1881

When the Civil War started, Garfield volunteered to fight, joining the Union side. He was first given the task of securing Kentucky. He was successful with this assignment and soon rose through the ranks. After the war, Garfield returned to Ohio where he entered politics and, as he had done on the field of battle, rose through the ranks. As the 1880 Presidential Election approached, he decided to run for the nation's highest office, the presidency.

President Garfield was shot in a train station and later died from his wounds.

James A. Garfield won the Election of 1880 and took the oath of office on March 4, 1881. He stated in his inaugural address that it was important for African-Americans to be treated as full citizens and that illiteracy was a huge problem in America. Tragically, on July 2nd of that year, while President Garfield was walking through a train station, he was shot twice by a man who was upset for not getting a government job. The wounded president was unable to make a full recovery and died a few months later.

| 1881 | 1881 | 1881 | 1881 |
|---|---|---|---|
| James A. Garfield takes office | Anti-Jewish riot takes place in Jerusalem | Frederick Douglas is appointed recorder of deeds for Washington, D.C. | Clara Barton founds the American Red Cross |

James Garfield won one of the most important minor battles of the Civil War when he defeated Confederate General Humphery Marshall in Eastern Kentucky. With only 1,100 men, Garfield pushed the Confederate force of 5,000 out of the state.

———————

The Tuskegee Institute (now known as Tuskegee University) was founded in Tuskegee, Alabama, in 1881. With the help of Booker T. Washington, the school became a pillar of education for many African-Americans who were being discriminated against because of the color of their skins.

Booker T. Washington

Clara Barton was a humanitarian who helped Civil War soldiers as early as 1861. After the war, she visited Europe and was introduced to the Red Cross organization. She later returned to the states and, in 1881, established the American Red Cross.

For over a century, the American Red Cross has been helping millions of people during times of war and natural disasters. It is best known for conducting blood drives and for providing food and medical attention to those in need.

## PRESIDENT QUIZ

### WHO AM I?

1825 - 1829

Page 16

### TRIVIA

Who caught a cold and died shortly after becoming president?

Page 22

"If wrinkles must be written on our brows, let them not be written upon the heart. The spirit should never grow old."

— James A. Garfield

| 1881 | 1881 | 1881 | 1881 |
|---|---|---|---|
| President Garfield is shot twice | Booker T. Washington helps establish the Tuskegee Institute | Ailing President Garfield is moved to Jersey Shore | President Garfield dies |

# #21  Chester A. Arthur
## (1881 - 1885)

Born: October 5, 1829
Died: November 18, 1886

Chester A. Arthur was born in Vermont in 1829. He attended prep schools and later graduated with a degree from Union College in New York. Afterwards, he became a teacher and then a successful lawyer. In New York City, he helped end segregation of the city's transit systems.

During the Civil War, Arthur held high posts in the New York militia. He returned to his law practice after the war and then became Collector of the Port of New York, a very powerful position at that time. When it came time for the 1880 Presidential Election, the Republican Party chose James A. Garfield as its presidential candidate and Arthur as its vice presidential candidate. The two men won the election and Arthur became the nation's newest vice president.

Chester A. Arthur became president after President Garfield passed away from a gunshot wound and, in a short period, nearly all of Garfield's cabinet members resigned. Only Todd Lincoln, son of President Lincoln, remained. One of Arthur's greatest achievements was getting a law passed that made people take written examinations to prove they were worthy of certain government jobs. But despite that, he couldn't secure the Republican Party's nomination in the next presidential election and retired from politics.

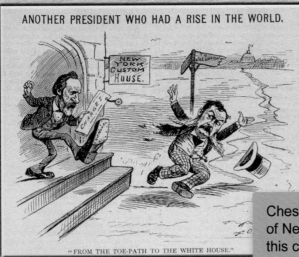

ANOTHER PRESIDENT WHO HAD A RISE IN THE WORLD.

"FROM THE TOE-PATH TO THE WHITE HOUSE."

Chester A. Arthur was appointed Collector of the Port of New York by President Grant in 1871. In 1878, as this cartoon depicts, President Rutherford B. Hayes removed him from this powerful position.

| 1881 | 1881 | 1882 | 1882 |
|---|---|---|---|
| Chester A. Arthur takes office | The shootout at the OK Corral occurs in Arizona | The electric iron is patented | The Hatfied-McCoy Feud begins in the Appalachian Mountains |

The Hatfield-McCoy Feud began when President Arthur was in office. The Hatfield clan (mostly from West Virginia) and the McCoy clan (mostly from Kentucky) didn't like each other for a host of reasons. They were predominantly on opposite sides during the Civil War (the Hatfields favored the Confederacy and the McCoys favored the Union) and they had a few encounters in court. On August 7, 1882, feelings between the two families took a turn for the worst when members of both families showed up at a Kentucky voting site during an election. Words were traded and then knives and gunshots. Ellison Hatfield died after being stabbed 26 times and shot. Following his death, the three McCoy's that were believed to have been responsible were seized, tied to bushes, and shot to death by members of the Hatfield family. The feud was on.

The Hatfield-McCoy Feud led to the deaths of more than a dozen members of the two families and gained national attention. The governors of West Virginia and Kentucky were compelled to call up their state militias to restore order and West Virginia's governor once threatened to have his militia invade Kentucky! The feud ended in 1891 when the families agreed to stop fighting each other.

Members of the Hatfield family pose for a picture.

Speaking of feuds, the "Gunfight at the OK Corral" took place when President Arthur was in office.

## PRESIDENT QUIZ

### WHO AM I?

1929 - 1933

Page 66

### TRIVIA

Who became president after Theodore Roosevelt left office?

Page 58

"The extravagant expenditure of public money is an evil not to be measured by the value of that people who are taxed for it."

— Chester A. Arthur

| 1883 | 1884 | 1884 | 1885 |
|------|------|------|------|
| "Buffalo Bill" Cody performs his first Wild West Show | Alaska becomes a U.S. Territory | An African-American is elected chairman of the Republican Convention | America's first appendectomy is performed |

# #22 Grover Cleveland
## (1885 - 1889)

Grover Cleveland was born in 1837 in Caldwell, New Jersey, and later moved with his family to New York where he spent much of his childhood. After his father died, Cleveland supported his family by becoming a teacher. Later, he moved to Buffalo and worked for his uncle. Here, he met influential men, studied hard, and became a lawyer.

Born: March 18, 1837
Died: June 24, 1908

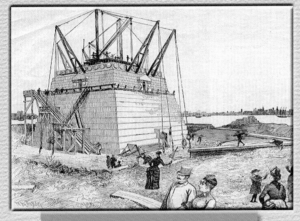

Building begins on the pedestal for the Statue of Liberty in 1885.

During the Civil War, Cleveland continued to practice law and support his mother and younger sisters. He was elected sheriff of New York's Erie County when he was only thirty-three years old and personally carried out the executions of several men. Afterwards, his popularity grew. He became mayor of Buffalo and then New York's governor. When it came time for the 1884 Presidential Election, Cleveland threw his hat into the ring and secured the Democratic Party's nomination.

Grover Cleveland won the Election of 1884 and took the oath of office in 1885. As president, he worked to reform the federal government. He created the Interstate Commerce Commission; modernized the navy; and, for the most part, hired people to government positions based upon their merit and not based upon their party loyalties.

During President Cleveland's second year in office, he married twenty-one year old Frances Folsom, the youngest First Lady ever! However, her stay in the White House was short-lived because, in the next election, President Cleveland got the most popular votes but not the most electoral votes.

| 1885 | 1885 | 1886 | 1886 |
|------|------|------|------|
| Grover Cleveland takes office | The Statue of Liberty (a gift from France) arrives in New York | Anti-Chinese violence escalates in Seattle | Chief Geronimo surrenders to the U.S. |

The United States received the Statue of Liberty from France during President Cleveland's first term. The gift (located on Liberty Island in New York Harbor) was dedicated on October 28,1886, and is a robed female figure that represents Libertas, the Roman goddess of freedom. Initially, the statue was intended to serve as a lighthouse, but the light of the torch was too dim to be useful. Also, when it was built, the statue had a dull copper color. However, shortly after 1900, a green patina (caused by oxidation of the statue's covering) grew over the statue's surface, giving us its current green appearance. Still, despite its change of color, the Statue of Liberty remains unchanged as a symbol of freedom, especially to the many boatloads of immigrants that saw the towering figure when they entered the U.S. through New York Harbor.

After President Cleveland's defeat in the Election of 1888, First Lady Frances Cleveland told the White House staff that she would be returning in four years.

As history would show, she was correct.

The Baby Ruth candy bar was supposedly named after President Cleveland's daughter, Ruth. It was not named after Babe Ruth, the baseball player.

## PRESIDENT QUIZ

### WHO AM I?

1841 – 1841

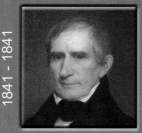

Page 22

### TRIVIA

Who became president after Richard Nixon resigned?

Page 80

"A government for the people must depend on the success on the intelligence, the morality, the justice, and the interest of the people themselves."
— Grover Cleveland

| 1887 | 1887 | 1888 | 1889 |
|------|------|------|------|
| Helen Keller learns "water" from her teacher | Mighty Casey strikes out against the New York Giants | Frederick Douglas is nominated for president | The first "computer" is patented |

# #23 Benjamin Harrison
## (1889 - 1893)

Benjamin Harrison was born in Ohio in 1833. He was the grandson of President William Henry Harrison and the second of nine children. After graduating from college, he began studying law. He also married Caroline Scott in 1853 and, a year later, began practicing law in Indiana.

Born: August 20, 1833
Died: March 13, 1901

During the Civil War, Harrison joined the Union Army. He signed up, served with William T. Sherman, and climbed to the rank of Brigadier General. After the war, he returned to Indiana where he became a U.S. Senator. A few years later, in 1888, he became the Republican Party's suprise nominee for president.

In the Election of 1888, Benjamin Harrison defeated incumbent President Grover Cleveland to become America's newest president. This election was one of the rare occasions where the winner actually received fewer popular votes than his opponent.

As president, Harrison raised tariffs; gave pensions to disabled Civil War veterans; and passed the first federal law to curb powerful monopolies. In 1892, President Harrison lost his re-election bid to the same man he defeated in 1888 (President Grover Cleveland). He returned to his law practice after leaving office.

Before becoming president, Benjamin Harrison fought for the Union during the Civil War.

| 1889 | 1889 | 1890 | 1890 |
|------|------|------|------|
| Benjamin Harrison takes office | White settlers begin moving into the Oklahoma Territory | The U.S. Census counts 62.9 million Americans | Wyoming becomes the first state to give women the right to vote |

The Oklahoma Land Rush began at high noon on April 22, 1889. At that time, approximately 50,000 people rushed into areas of Oklahoma that were originally Indian Territory to stake their claims to the land. Still, some people broke the law by entering the open territory early and hiding. Then, when the legal time of entry had passed, these individuals (called 'Sooners') came out of hiding and staked their claims on prime land. Over time, more and more settlers moved to Oklahoma, thus paving the way for Oklahoma to become a state in 1907.

Years before the 1889 Oklahoma Land Rush, all of Oklahoma was Indian Territory and off limits to U.S. settlement. However, the U.S. Government forced the Indians residing in Oklahoma to sign new treaties that shrank the Indian Territory. The Oklahoma land that the Indians gave up became the new property of the U.S. Government and the Government, in turn, opened a large chunk of the newly-acquired land for development to predominantly white settlers.

The Indian tribes living in Oklahoma at the time of the Land Rush were originally from areas east of the Mississippi River. These tribes (which included the Creek, Choctaw, Cherokee, Chickasaw, and Seminole nations) were relocated during the 1830's because they didn't want to assimilate and become American citizens.

The Oklahoma Land Rush begins.

## PRESIDENT QUIZ

### WHO AM I?

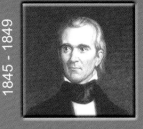

1845 - 1849

Page 26

### TRIVIA

Which president died after being shot in a train station?

Page 44

"We Americans have no commission from God to police the world."

— Benjamin Harrison

| 1891 | 1891 | 1892 | 1893 |
|------|------|------|------|
| American Express issues its first traveler's checks | The game of basketball is created in Massachusetts | The General Electric Company is formed | Hawaii becomes a republic after deposing its queen |

# #24 Grover Cleveland
## (1893 - 1897)

Remember this guy? It's Grover Cleveland again, both the 22nd and 24th President of the United States. If you don't remember much about his early life you can turn a few pages back and read all about it. Oh, and one more thing that wasn't mentioned before: Grover Cleveland is a comeback kid!

After being defeated by Harrison in the 1888 Presidential Election, Cleveland and his wife moved to New York City. Cleveland joined a law firm and saw the birth of his first child, Ruth. He also wrote an open letter dealing with politics that boosted his popularity. When it was time for another presidential election, the Democratic Party decided to back Cleveland again.

Born: March 18, 1837
Died: June 24, 1908

The Election of 1892 featured the same two candidates from the previous election (Grover Cleveland and Benjamin Harrison), but the outcome was different. This time, Cleveland was the winner. Shortly after taking office, he was faced with bank failures; an economic depression; and labor strikes among workers who were unhappy with low wages and twelve-hour workdays. When it came time for the next election, President Cleveland declined his party's nomination and retired.

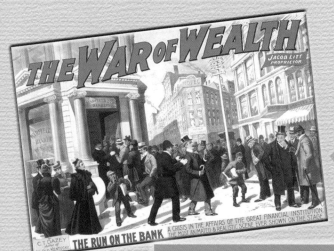

The Panic of 1893 triggered bank failures. This poster was for a play written about the crisis.

| 1893 | 1893 | 1893 | 1894 |
|------|------|------|------|
| Grover Cleveland takes office | The Panic of 1893 triggers bank failures | Many Chinese are deported from San Francisco | Over 130,000 miners in Ohio go on strike for pay increases |

In 1894, "Coxey's Army" marched to Washington, D.C., to oppose the Federal Government's handling of the depression. The "army" was comprised mostly of unemployed workers, led by Jacob Coxey, and numbered about 100 men when it first began its journey from Massillon, Ohio. Nearly a month later, the protesters reached the Capital and their numbers swelled to nearly 6,000 people. Coxey and other leaders were arrested for walking on the grass of the U.S. Capital and the protest came to a quick halt.

Coxey's Army is on the move, marching to Washington, D.C.

NWEAL ARMY LEAVING BRIGHTWOOD CAMP.

In winning the Election of 1892, President Cleveland set himself apart from all U.S. presidents (both before and after) by becoming the only president to leave office and later return.

After taking office for this his second time, President Cleveland was faced with the Panic of 1893 and what was to become a six-year economic depression. The crisis was worse than any America had ever seen before. Nearly 20% of the workforce was left without work and many Americans who couldn't meet their mortgage payments simply walked away from their homes.

"Public officers are the servants and agents of the people, to execute the laws which the people have made."

— Grover Cleveland

| 1894 | 1895 | 1895 | 1896 |
|------|------|------|------|
| The American Railway Union goes on strike | The game of volleyball is invented in Massachusetts | A moving picture projector is patented | The X-ray machine is demonstrated in the U.S. |

# #25 William McKinley
## (1897 - 1901)

William McKinley was born in Ohio in 1843. He fought with the Union Army during the Civil War and obtained the rank of captain. After the war, he became a lawyer and opened a law practice in Canton, Ohio. McKinley married Ida Saxon in 1871. They had two daughters that died before seeing the age of five.

McKinley also served as a prosecuting attorney in Ohio and became active in politics when he campaigned for his old commander, Rutherford B. Hayes, who was running for Ohio's governor at the time. In turn, Hayes helped McKinley get elected to the U.S. House of Representatives. A few years later, McKinley was elected Ohio's governor and, when his term was finished, he set sights on the White House.

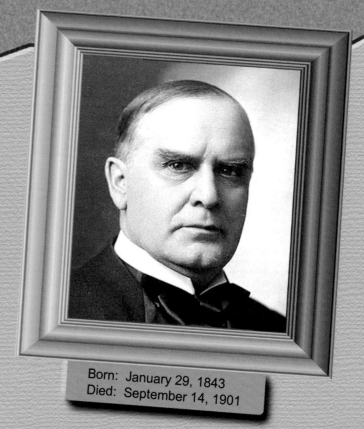

Born: January 29, 1843
Died: September 14, 1901

President McKinley was assassinated in 1901.

William McKinley became president by winning the Election of 1896. In office, he led the U.S. to victory in the Spanish-American War. He also pushed to make American producers more valuable in the world. On the home front, President McKinley supported civil rights to all African-Americans, but he was unwilling to use federal power to stop many injustices that were taking place in the nation. He was re-elected to a second term in 1900 and was assassinated less than a year later.

| 1897 | 1897 | 1898 | 1898 |
|---|---|---|---|
| William McKinley takes office | Nineteen striking miners are killed by police in Lattimer, PA | The USS Maine explodes and sinks | The Spanish-American War begins |

Future President Theodore Roosevelt and his "Rough Riders" fought during the Spanish-American War. Here they are pictured after a victory in Cuba.

The unexplained explosion of the USS Maine in Havana Harbor in 1898 was one spark that led to the Spanish-American War. Many Americans believed Spain was responsible for sinking the ship.

## PRESIDENT QUIZ

### WHO AM I?

1923 - 1929

Page 64

### TRIVIA

Who became the "Free Soil" Party's nominee for president in 1848?

Page 20

"War should never be entered upon until every agency of peace has failed."

— William McKinley

| 1898 | 1899 | 1900 | 1901 |
|------|------|------|------|
| The machine gun is first used in battle | The Spanish-American War ends | The U.S. Census counts 76.2 million Americans | President McKinley is assassinated |

# #26 Theodore Roosevelt
## (1901 - 1909)

Theodore Roosevelt was born in 1858 in New York. As a child, he was asthmatic and often had to sleep either propped up in bed or slouching in a chair. At the age of seven, he developed a love for zoology (the study of animals) that stayed with him the rest of his life. He also took boxing lessons to combat his poor physical condition.

Born: October 27, 1858
Died: January 6, 1919

After graduating from Harvard College in 1880, Roosevelt underwent a physical examination and was instructed by his doctor to avoid strenuous activity due to serious heart problems. However, instead of finding a desk job, Roosevelt stayed on the move. He joined the U. S. Army and became a war hero riding with the calvary in the Spanish-American War. Shortly after leaving the army, he was elected New York's governor. He then became President McKinley's vice president.

This 1902 political cartoon shows Roosevelt refusing to shoot a bear held in captivity. The cartoon was based on a hunting trip Roosevelt took in Mississippi.

After President McKinley died, Theodore Roosevelt became president and a popular one at that. After completing McKinley's term, President Roosevelt was elected to two more and then retired. In office, he worked to curb the power of large corporations; passed legislation to ban misleading advertising; and began holding press briefings with reporters, something that was never done before. Four years after retiring, he came back and ran for the presidency again! This time, he ran under the new "Bull Moose" Party. Roosevelt lost this election and went back into retirement.

| 1901 | 1902 | 1903 | 1904 |
|------|------|------|------|
| Theodore Roosevelt takes office | The U.S. takes over construction of the Panama Canal | The Wright brothers fly the first successful airplane | The U.S. ends its occupation of Cuba |

In 1902, the U.S. took over the construction of the Panama Canal after the French abandoned the project because of high costs and having incurred over 20,000 deaths, mostly due to disease. When the canal was completed in 1914, the waterway created a vital link between the Atlantic and Pacific Oceans.

---

Yes, the "teddy bear" gets its name from President Theodore Roosevelt.

After learning the president refused to shoot a tied-up bear, Morris Michtom began making stuffed bear cub toys. He labeled them as "Teddy's bear" to help sales and rest is history.

On December 17, 1903, Orville and Wilbur Wright flew into history when their airplane successfully took to the air in North Carolina. The brothers were from Ohio, but they selected North Carolina as the place for their flight because of the favorable wind conditions there.

The flight only lasted twelve seconds, but it was enough to propel the world into a new age!

## PRESIDENT QUIZ

### WHO AM I?

1989 - 1993

Page 86

### TRIVIA

Who was president during the "9/11" terrorist attacks?

Page 90

"A vote is like a rifle; its usefulness depends upon the character of the user."

— Theodore Roosevelt

| 1907 | 1908 | 1908 | 1909 |
|------|------|------|------|
| Automatic washers and dryers are available to public | The Gideon Bible is placed into its first hotel room | Henry Ford introduces the Model T automobile | The first U.S. fleet to circle the globe returns to port |

# #27 William H. Taft
## (1909 - 1913)

Born: September 15, 1857
Died: March 8, 1930

William Taft was born in Ohio in 1857. He graduated from both Yale College and the Cincinnati Law School. He then began a legal career which helped him to become a judge to the Ohio Superior Court; the U.S. Solicitor General; and a judge on the U.S. Court of Appeals.

Taft also served as the Governor-General of the Philippines from 1901 to 1903. He was later offered a seat on the Supreme Court, a position he aspired to attain, but he turned it down to help the Philippines reach the capacity to govern itself. A year later, in 1904, he became President Roosevelt's Secretary of War. When President Roosevelt decided not to run for the presidency in 1908, Taft became the Republican Party's choice.

With the backing of President Roosevelt, William H. Taft easily won the Election of 1908 and became America's newest president. In office, he created a postal service system for delivering mail within the states and supported a federal income tax. When the next election came around, he and Roosevelt (who decided that he wanted to be president again) wrestled for control of the Republican Party. Taft was able to secure the Republican Party's nomination which prompted Roosevelt to march off and start his own political party, the "Bull Moose" Party. Both men ended up losing the Election of 1912 to Woodrow Wilson, a Democrat.

In this 1912 political ad, President Taft is billed as a president deserving a second term and Theodore Roosevelt is portrayed as undeserving of a third term.

| 1909 | 1909 | 1910 | 1910 |
|------|------|------|------|
| William H. Taft takes office | The first NAACP conference is held in the U.S. | The U.S. Census counts 92.2 million Americans | Earth passes through the tail of Halley's Comet |

In 1910, Halley's comet made its usual 75 to 76-year appearance in our solar system and (with the help of expansive newspaper coverage) fueled fear in many that the end of the world may be near. What didn't help matters was the fact the comet passed so close that the Earth actually passed through the comet's 24-million-mile-long tail for six hours! Telescope sales were astronomical; President Taft made a visit to the U.S. Naval Observatory to get a closer look; and hotels in large cities were filled with people wanting to get to their high roof tops to see the rare visitor. After the earth passed through the comet's tail, many people breathed a sigh of relief and went back to their normal business. The planet wasn't doomed after all.

American author Samuel Clemens (also known as Mark Twain) was born when Halley's comet visited our solar system in 1835. In 1909, just one year prior to the comet's return, he said, "I came in with Halley's Comet in 1835. It is coming again next year, and I expect to go out with it." His expectations were correct. Shortly after the comet reached perihelion, Mark Twain died.

Samuel Clemens, author

The RMS Titanic hit an iceberg and sank in the Atlantic Ocean in April of 1912.

1,517 people died in frigid waters.

# PRESIDENT QUIZ

## WHO AM I?

1841 - 1845

Page 24

## TRIVIA

Who became president after Warren G. Harding died in 1923?

Page 64

"We live in the stage of politics, where legislators seem to regard the passage of laws as much more important than the results of their enforcement."

— William H. Taft

| 1911 | 1912 | 1912 | 1913 |
|---|---|---|---|
| Let's cook! Crisco shortening hits the stores | The Titanic sinks in the Atlantic Ocean | Theodore Roosevelt starts the "Bull Moose" Party | Federal income tax is once again the law of the land |

# #28 Woodrow Wilson
## (1913 - 1921)

Woodrow Wilson was born in Virginia in 1856. He didn't learn to read until he was over ten years old, probably due to dyslexia. Wilson learned shorthand to compensate for his reading deficiency and went on to become a lawyer. In 1883, he left his law practice to study history and political science to prep himself for a career in politics.

Born: December 28, 1856
Died: February 3, 1924

Woodrow Wilson was president during World War I.

Between 1883 and 1902, Wilson wrote and spoke about what he saw as flaws in America's political system. He then became president of Princeton University and, in 1910, the governor of New Jersey. As governor, he introduced worker's compensation and revamped many political processes. With support for him growing, Wilson decided to make a run for the nation's highest office. He became the Democratic Party's nominee in 1912.

Woodrow Wilson won the Election of 1912 and, four years later, the Election of 1916. As president, he became a leader in the Progressive Era, a period of reform. In office, he worked with Congress to pass the 18th Amendment (which prohibited the sale of alcoholic beverages) and the 19th Amendment (which gave women the right to vote). He also led America through World War I. President Wilson suffered a stroke that left him in a wheelchair for a while and didn't seek a third term due to his declining health.

Many thought World War I would be the "war to end all wars." They were wrong.

| 1913 | 1914 | 1914 | 1917 |
|---|---|---|---|
| Woodrow Wilson takes office | The Panama Canal opens | World War I begins in Europe | Russia's Communist Revolution begins |

The United States entered World War I during the third year of the conflict in 1917. Joining the Allied Powers of France, the British Empire, Russia, Italy, and various other smaller nations, American soldiers traveled to Europe to fight against the Central Powers of Germany, Austria-Hungry, the Ottoman Empire, and Bulgaria. The introduction of U.S. soldiers helped break a stalemate in the trenches of France and ultimately led to an Allied victory. In the war's aftermath, the German people had to make restitutions for war damages that led to hyperinflation, a hungry German populous, and the eventual rise of Adolf Hitler who promised a better and stronger Germany. Though the U.S. helped stop the fighting in 1918, the seeds for World War II were sown.

Nearly 120,000 American soldiers died during the short time that the U.S. fought during World War I. Another 200,000 were wounded.

During World War I, President Wilson passed laws that suppressed America's freedom of speech. Many citizens were imprisoned for saying they disagreed with America's involvement in the war and others were even jailed for criticizing the Red Cross and YMCA!

## PRESIDENT QUIZ

### WHO AM I?

1817 - 1825

Page 14

### TRIVIA

Which president served two non-consecutive terms?

Page 48

"Liberty has never come from Government. Liberty has always come from the subjects of it. The history of liberty is the history of limitations of governmental power, not the increase of it."

— Woodrow Wilson

| 1919 | 1920 | 1920 | 1920 |
|---|---|---|---|
| World War I ends | The League of Nations is created, but the U.S. doesn't join | The U.S. Census counts 106 million Americans | The 19th Amendment gives women the right to vote |

# #29 Warren G. Harding
## (1921 - 1923)

Warren Harding was born in 1865 in Ohio. After college, he and some friends bought the weakest newspaper in Marion, Ohio, and went to work. Harding became very exhausted in his new business and spent time recovering at a sanitarium. A few years later, he married Florence DeWolfe.

Born: November 2, 1865
Died: August 2, 1923

With his newspaper and his wife supporting him, Harding was elected to the Ohio State Senate. He later became Ohio's lieutenant governor and lost in his attempt to become governor. After this setback, he bounced back and became a U.S. Senator. He served in this position for several years and became the Republican's Party's choice for president in 1920.

Warren G. Harding won the Election of 1920 by defeating a fellow Ohioan. During the campaign, he promised "a return to normalcy," which meant, in part, that he didn't want America involved in international affairs, especially if it meant war. In office, he established what became known as the Department of Veterans Affairs to help war veterans in need and he helped lead America out of an economic depression. Tragically, Harding died of a heart attack about midway through his term.

The 1919 Chicago White Sox became known as the Chicago "Black Sox" because some of its players took money to lose the World Series. In 1921, the accused players had to answer to charges in a highly-publicized court trial.

| 1921 | 1921 | 1921 | 1922 |
|---|---|---|---|
| Warren G. Harding takes office | Albert Einstein talks about his Theory of Relativity | The Chicago "Black Sox" baseball scandal goes to court | Many new American radio stations hit the airwaves |

After the Nineteenth Amendment to the U.S. Constitution was ratified in August of 1920, the Presidential Election of 1920 became unique because, for the first time in American history, women nationwide were given the right to vote! The leading candidates during this election were Warren G. Harding (Republican) and James M. Cox (Democrat).

During the campaign, Harding took advantage of the public's growing hostility toward Woodrow Wilson, the Democratic president. Many Americans didn't want the U.S. to join the Wilson-sponsored League of Nations; the U.S. economy was in a recession; and large groups of Americans of European descent were outraged at Wilson's wartime policies. As a result, the Republicans won the election with Harding capturing 404 electoral votes (60% of the popular vote) and Cox gathering only 127 electoral votes (34% of the popular vote).

On December 23, 1921, President Harding commuted the jail sentence of American socialist Eugene Debs, effective Christmas Day. Debs was a union leader who was openly opposed to U.S. involvement in World War I when Woodrow Wilson was president. He was arrested in 1918 and imprisoned for sedition in 1919. President Wilson said that Debs was a "traitor to this country" for speaking out against American involvement in the war, but President Harding perceived the ten-year sentence as being too harsh and let Debs go free.

In addition to being a union leader, Eugene Debs was also active in politics. He ran for president as a socialist in 1900, 1904, 1908, and 1920. He received more and more votes with each election but never more than 6% of the total cast. He was still in jail during his 1920 run!

Eugene Debs

## PRESIDENT QUIZ

### WHO AM I?

1789 - 1797

Page 6

### TRIVIA

Who became president after James Garfield was assassinated?

Page 46

"In the beginning the Old World scoffed at our experiment; today our foundations of political and social belief stand unshaken, a precious inheritance to ourselves, an inspiring example of freedom and civilization to all mankind."

— Warren G. Harding

| 1922 | 1922 | 1923 | 1923 |
|---|---|---|---|
| The U.S. launches its first aircraft carrier | King Tut's tomb is discovered in Egypt | Time Magazine hits the newsstands | President Harding dies |

# #30 Calvin Coolidge
## (1923 - 1929)

Calvin Coolidge was born on July 4th (Independence Day), 1872, in Vermont. When he was twelve, his mother died. In 1898, Coolidge opened a law office in Massachusetts and gained a reputation as a diligent attorney. As a result, many local businesses utilized his services. Coolidge then became active in politics and married.

Coolidge served the city of Northampton in a number of positions before winning a seat to the Massachusetts House of Representatives. Here, he was known as a progressive Republican, supporting women's rights to vote and the direct election of U.S. senators who, at the time, were elected by state legislatures. He eventually climbed the political ladder and became vice president of the United States.

Born: July 4, 1872
Died: January 5, 1933

Calvin Coolidge became president after President Warren G. Harding died and then went on to win the Election of 1924. As president during the "Roaring Twenties," he and Congress lowered taxes to the point where over 95% of all American's didn't pay income tax! His popularity, however, sagged due to his slow response in sending federal aid to help those affected by the Great Mississippi Flood of 1927. President Coolidge didn't seek the presidency in 1928 and retired when his final term ended.

"The Great Mississippi Flood of 1927" led to the deaths of over 200 people and caused over $400 million in damages.

| 1923 | 1924 | 1925 | 1925 |
|---|---|---|---|
| Calvin Coolidge takes office | Edwin Hubble announces existence of other galaxies | Tennessee outlaws the teaching of evolution in schools | The Ku Klux Klan marches in Washington, D.C. |

President Coolidge signed the Immigration Act of 1924. This federal law limited the number of immigrants who could be admitted into the U.S. to no more than 2% of people from that country who were already living in America as of 1890. However, one somewhat discriminatory aspect of the law forbade immigration from the "undesirable" Asian-Pacific Triangle countries (Japan, China, and other Southeast Asian nations). The new law also set no limits on immigration from Latin America countries.

The electoral map from the 1924 Presidential Election gave the appearance of a division between southern states and the rest of the Union. Republican Calvin Coolidge carried most northern states and all the western states. Democrat John W. Davis carried Oklahoma and the eleven southern states that fought for the Confederacy during the Civil War. Robert La Follette ran as the Progressive Party's candidate and carried Wisconsin.

Charles Lindbergh

Aviation showed its advancement during President Coolidge's last term in office when Charles Lindbergh, a 25-year-old U.S. Air Mail pilot, became the first person to make a solo non-stop flight from New York to Paris in an airplane. For his efforts, he won the Orteig Prize of $25,000 and a place in history. His flight was made in 1927.

## PRESIDENT QUIZ

### WHO AM I?

1909 - 1913

Page 58

### TRIVIA

Who was the first president of the United States?

Page 6

"Little progress can be made by merely attempting to repress what is evil.
Our great hope lies in developing what is good"

— Calvin Coolidge

| 1926 | 1927 | 1928 | 1928 |
|------|------|------|------|
| "Talking" movies premiere in U.S. theaters | Charles Lindbergh makes historic flight across the Atlantic Ocean | Walt Disney's Mickey Mouse debuts for the first time | A hurricane kills at least 2,500 in Florida |

# #31  Herbert Hoover
## (1929 - 1933)

Herbert Hoover was born in Iowa in 1874. At the age of nine, his parents died and he became an orphan. He was bounced among a few relatives for a short time and ended up living with an uncle. In 1891, after attending night school, Hoover was admitted to Stanford University where he graduated with a degree in geology.

Hoover went to work in many countries throughout the world. During World War I, he led a few hundred volunteers who helped get Americans home from Europe. He also led relief efforts to help over nine million war victims. When he returned home, he became active in the U.S. Government by becoming the Secretary of Commerce. He became very popular when he led flood relief efforts after the Mississippi River broke its banks in 1927.

Born: August 10, 1874
Died: October 20, 1964

Herbert Hoover became popular for leading relief efforts during the 1927 Mississippi Flood.

When President Coolidge decided not to run for a second term in 1928, Herbert Hoover jumped at the chance and won. In office, he confidently stated, "We in America today are nearer to the final triumph over poverty than ever before in the history of any land." Unfortunately, a few months later, the great Stock Market Crash of 1929 occurred. When it came time for the next election, almost 25% of Americans were out of work and President Hoover was easily defeated.

| 1929 | 1929 | 1929 | 1930 |
|------|------|------|------|
| Herbert Hoover takes office | The U.S. introduces smaller-sized currency | A Stock Market Crash precedes The Great Depression | The U.S. Census counts 122 million Americans |

The Great Depression began shortly after the Stock Market Crash of 1929. In the years to follow, families would have to adjust to hard times.

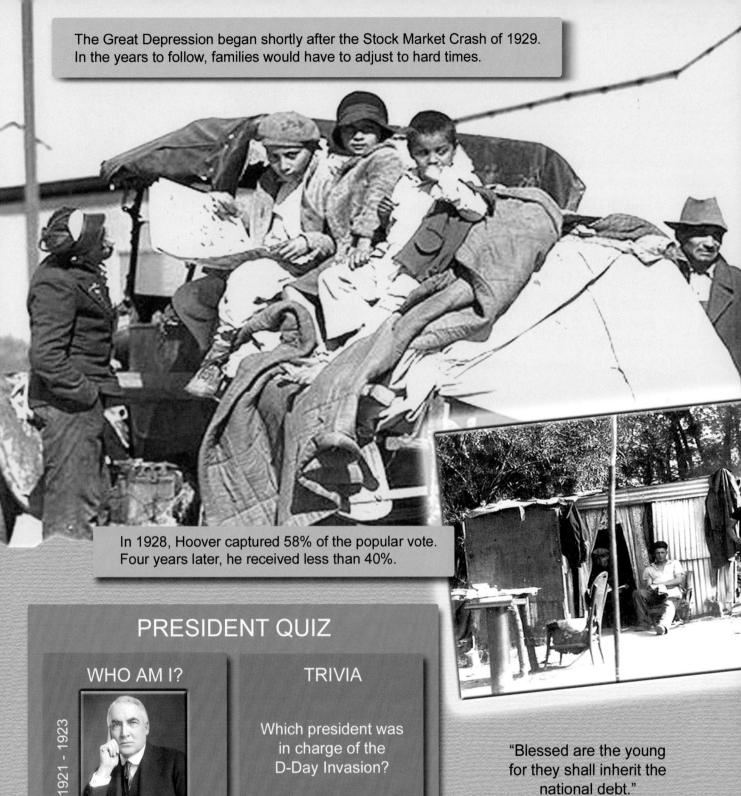

In 1928, Hoover captured 58% of the popular vote. Four years later, he received less than 40%.

## PRESIDENT QUIZ

### WHO AM I?

1921 - 1923

Page 62

### TRIVIA

Which president was in charge of the D-Day Invasion?

Page 72

"Blessed are the young for they shall inherit the national debt."

— Herbert Hoover

**1930**
The "planet" Pluto is confirmed to exist

**1931**
The "Star-Spangled Banner" becomes America's national anthem

**1932**
Twenty-month-old Charles Lindbergh, Jr., is kidnapped and killed

**1932**
Mobster Al Capone is convicted of tax evasion

# #32 Franklin D. Roosevelt
## (1933 - 1945)

Franklin Delano Roosevelt was born in 1882 to one of the wealthiest families in New York State. By the time he turned twenty-six, he had become a lawyer and a husband. Over the next few years, he served as a state senator and the Secretary of the Navy. Roosevelt resigned from the Navy in 1920.

Born: January 30, 1882
Died: April 12, 1945

In 1920, Roosevelt became the Democratic Party's vice presidential candidate for the White House. He and James Cox lost this election to Warren Harding. One year later, things got tougher for Roosevelt. He became paralyzed from the waist down due to illness. Still, despite his handicap, Roosevelt went on to become New York's governor and grew in popularity. When the Presidential Election of 1932 came around, he was the Democratic Party's choice for president.

The USS Arizona sinks in Pearl Harbor after Japan attacked the U.S. Naval Fleet stationed there. This act thrust America into World War II.

In the midst of the Great Depression, Franklin Delano Roosevelt won the Election of 1932 and enacted programs to help the economy and get people back to work. His soaring popularity then carried him to victories in the Presidential Elections of 1936, 1940, and 1944. That's right, Roosevelt won four elections in a row! While contending with the poor economy, he had to lead the U.S. during World War II. Sadly, shortly after his fourth term began, he died of a stroke.

| 1933 | 1933 | 1936 | 1939 |
|------|------|------|------|
| Franklin D. Roosevelt takes office | Prohibition comes to an end | Olympian Jesse Owens wins four gold medals in Berlin, Germany | World War II begins with Germany's invasion of Poland |

Adolf Hitler began World War II in 1939 when his German forces invaded Poland. Initially, the U.S. stayed out of the conflict, but things changed after Japan attacked the U.S. Fleet at Pearl Harbor, Hawaii. Congress quickly declared war on both Japan and Germany, and President Roosevelt helped lead America and its allies to victory.

Jesse Owens was an American athlete who won four gold medals at the 1936 Olympic Games in Berlin, Germany. At that time, Adolf Hitler was Germany's leader and he was using propaganda to promote his concept of Aryan racial superiority. Sadly, despite Owen's being an African-American, many Germans bought into Hitler's radical ideology.

Did you know that Franklin D. Roosevelt was the fifth cousin of President Theodore Roosevelt?

Albert Einstein was born in Germany and fled when he realized that Adolf Hitler and the Nazis Party were planning to persecute those of Jewish heritage. He soon came to the U.S. where he became an instrumental figure in developing the Atomic Bomb. He also became an American citizen in 1940 and expressed his appreciation for this country by saying of it, "No one humbles himself before another person or class."

## PRESIDENT QUIZ

### WHO AM I?

1993 - 2001

Page 88

### TRIVIA

Who was the only president to resign from office?

Page 78

"Yesterday, December 7th, 1941, a date which will live in infamy, the United States of America was suddenly and deliberately attacked by naval and air forces of the Empire of Japan"

— Franklin D. Roosevelt

**1940**
The U.S. Census counts 132 million Americans

**1941**
The U.S. enters World War II after Japan's attack

**1944**
The U.S. and allies launch D-Day invasion of Western Europe

**1945**
President Roosevelt dies

# #33  Harry S. Truman
## (1945 - 1953)

Born: May 8, 1884
Died: December 26, 1972

Harry S. Truman was born in Missouri in 1884. He developed interests in reading, history, and music at a young age. After high school, he slept in "hobo camps" while working as a timekeeper for the railroad. He left that job, became a clerk for a while, and then went to Europe to fight in World War I. The war brought out Truman's leadership abilities.

Truman returned to Missouri after the war and married Bess Wallace. Truman then worked in several government positions and became popular in his state. Finally, in 1934, he hit it big by winning a U.S. Senate seat. He worked tirelessly in this position and, in 1944, earned the confidence of the Democratic Party. Truman was selected to replace Henry Wallace as President Roosevelt's vice president.

Harry S. Truman became president after President Roosevelt died and, to bring a quick end to World War II, approved of the atomic bombing of Japan. After the war, he led America through the transition back into a peace-time economy; played a role in the creation of Israel; and conducted the Berlin Airlift when Russia blocked access to Western-held sections of the German city. He went on to win the Election of 1948 and sent troops to fight in the Korean War. When his term was completed in 1953, he retired.

Shortly after Truman became president, he approved dropping two atomic bombs on Japan in the hopes of shortening the war and saving many American lives. His hopes were correct. The war came to a quick end.

| 1945 | 1945 | 1945 | 1945 |
|------|------|------|------|
| Harry S. Truman becomes president | The U.S. drops two atomic bombs on Japan | World War II comes to an end | The United Nations is created with fifty-one members |

The end of World War II came shortly after the U.S. dropped two atomic bombs on Japan. The first was dropped on August 6, 1945, on the city of Hiroshima. The explosion and subsequent radiation from the blast killed nearly 200,000 people. Three days later, another atomic bomb was dropped on the city of Nagasaki where it was estimated that 100,000 people were killed. When the severity and power of America's new weapon was finally realized, Japan's leadership unconditionally surrendered and the war came to a halt. To this day, the debate over whether or not the U.S. should have used such a weapon is still heard; however, in Truman's day, it was firmly believed that America would have lost nearly one million soldiers trying to conquer Japan with conventional weapons.

The United Nations was created in 1945 in hopes of bringing peace to the world. The organization is now comprised of nearly all world nations and is headquartered in New York City. Though its hopes were for men to "beat their swords into plowshares", a biblical reference to peace, the United Nations hasn't been able to live up to such lofty aspirations.

In 1947, the United Nations voted to divide the land of Palestine between Jews and Arabs. Shortly afterwards, the new Jewish nation was attacked by an Arab alliance. The U.N. didn't step in to help, but Israel won the war anyway.

Israeli forces defend Jerusalem.

## PRESIDENT QUIZ

### WHO AM I?

1963 - 1969

Page 76

### TRIVIA

Which president was once an actor and a radio sportscaster?

Page 84

"Carry the battle to them. Don't let them bring it to you. Put them on the defensive and don't ever apologize for anything."

— Harry S. Truman

| 1948 | 1950 | 1950 | 1951 |
|------|------|------|------|
| The first tape recorder is sold | The U.S. Census counts 150 million Americans | America enters the three-year Korean War | The 22nd Amendment place term limits on presidents |

# #34 Dwight D. Eisenhower
## (1953 - 1961)

Dwight D. Eisenhower was born in Texas in 1890 and moved to Kansas with his family. He graduated from the West Point military academy in 1911 and trained tank crews during World War I. After the war, he remained in the military where he studied military history and tank warfare. When the U.S. entered World War II, he was a one-star general.

Born: October 14, 1890
Died: March 28, 1969

Eisenhower was in charge of the D-Day Invasion during World War II.

Dwight D. Eisenhower won the Election of 1952 and, four years later, the Election of 1956. In office, he continued many of President Roosevelt's New Deal programs; began work on the Interstate Highway System; sent military aid to South Vietnam; and led the overthrow of Iran's government. He also went to work integrating the capital's public school system to combat racial discrimination. After leaving office, the old general retired to a farm beside Pennsylvania's Gettysburg Battlefield.

During the war, Eisenhower helped plan Allied strategy in the Pacific, European, and African theaters of war. He was also put in charge of the D-Day Invasion and, after the war, the U.S. zone of conquered Germany. He later returned to America and, in 1952, retired from the military. In that same year, the "I Like Ike" campaign began and he became the Republican Party's nominee for president.

Eisenhower was a five-star general before becoming president.

| 1953 | 1954 | 1955 | 1956 |
|---|---|---|---|
| Dwight D. Eisenhower takes office | The first U.S. shopping mall opens in Michigan | Jonas Salk successfully tests a Polio vaccine | Martin Luther King's home is bombed |

When Russia launched the world's first satellite into space on October 4, 1957, many Americans feared their Cold War foe had a technological advantage that, if left unchecked, would spell doom to the U.S. nation. The American people voiced these fears and President Eisenhower responded by ordering the civilian rocket and satellite project (called "Vanguard") to move up its timetable and launch America's first satellite into space. Unfortunately, the December 6, 1957 attempt was a failure. Before a nationally-televised audience, the rocket rose four feet into the air, lost thrust, settled on the launch pad, and exploded. Americans were again disappointed, but their hopes were raised when the launch of Explorer I on January 31, 1958, proved a success. The U.S. was now in the space race.

The Soviet Union's first satellite was named Sputnik I. America's first satellite was named Explorer I. In this picture, Explorer I is launched into space atop the Juno I, a four-stage booster rocket.

Explorer I remained in orbit for more than twelve years. It crashed into the Pacific Ocean on March 19, 1970.

Did you know President Eisenhower declared racial discrimination a national security issue?

Communists were using the issue as a point of attack in their propaganda.

## PRESIDENT QUIZ

### WHO AM I?

1809 - 1817

Page 12

### TRIVIA

Which president was assassinated in 1901?

Page 54

"Don't join the book burners. Do not think you are going to conceal thoughts by concealing that they ever existed."
— Dwight D. Eisenhower

| 1958 | 1959 | 1960 | 1960 |
|---|---|---|---|
| The U.S. sends its first satellite into space | Fearing the worst, many homeowners build bomb shelters | The U.S. Census counts 179 million Americans | Francis Gary Power's U-2 spy plane is shot down by Russia |

# #35   John F. Kennedy
## (1961 - 1963)

John F. Kennedy was born in 1917 in Massachusetts and graduated from Harvard College with a degree in international affairs in 1941. As tensions were pointing to World War II, he volunteered for the U.S. Army but was rejected due to him having back problems. However, the U.S. Navy gladly took him aboard.

Born: May 29, 1917
Died: November 22, 1963

Kennedy became a hero during the war for his service aboard PT-109 (a torpedo patrol boat). After the war ended, he began his political career which included his election to the U.S. House of Representatives in 1946 and the U.S. Senate in 1952. Four years later, he nearly became the Democratic Party's Vice Presidential nominee; however, in 1960, he faired much better. He became his party's nominee for the nation's top prize, the presidency.

Kennedy became president by winning the 1960 Election. During his term, he confronted the spread of Communism throughout the world. The most memorable moment occurred when the U.S. stopped the Soviet Union from building nuclear missile sites in Cuba. President Kennedy was also credited for helping put man on the moon and promoting civil rights. Tragically, while he was in Dallas, Texas, campaigning to be re-elected, he was shot and killed by Lee Harvey Oswald. The nation mourned its loss.

John F. Kennedy commanded a PT boat during World War II. He received several medals for his service and obtained the rank of lieutenant.

| 1961 | 1961 | 1961 | 1961 |
|------|------|------|------|
| John F. Kennedy takes office | The Bay of Pigs fiasco takes place in Cuba | The Berlin Wall is constructed in Germany | Alan Shepard becomes the first American to enter space |

The Cuban Missile Crisis of 1962 is believed to have been the closest the world has come to World War III. The crisis came about as the result of the U.S. learning that the Soviet Union and the Communist nation of Cuba were building nuclear missile bases in Cuba. The U.S. promptly quarantined the island of Cuba and demanded that the Soviets dismantle the bases and remove any offensive weapons there. The Soviets countered by stating that any attempts by America to quarantine international waters would be an act of aggression that would lead to a nuclear war. The world feared the worst, but the conflict ended when the Soviets agreed to withdraw and the U.S. promised not to invade Cuba. The world sighed in relief.

President Kennedy went to West Berlin in 1963 and delivered a speech condemning the Soviet Union for building the Berlin Wall. The wall (a mass of concrete and barbed wire that separated Communist East Berlin from non-Communist West Berlin) was built to stop Germans caught in the Soviet-controlled areas from fleeing to the non-Communist world. Despite the president's visit, the wall stayed erected and divided some families for several decades to come. It wasn't until 1989 (following collapse of the Soviet Union) that the gates in the wall were opened to allow Germans from both sides to reunite.

Approximately 5,000 people escaped to West Berlin during the years when the Berlin Wall was in use and nearly 200 were killed trying. Some escaped by digging tunnels under the wall; others drove through security check points under a hail of bullet fire; and a few flew hot air balloons and ultralights over the barrier.

Martin Luther King, Jr., gave his "I Have a Dream" speech in 1963.

## PRESIDENT QUIZ

### WHO AM I?

2001 - 2009

Page 90

### TRIVIA

Who was the second president of the United States?

Page 8

"And so, my fellow Americans, ask not what your country can do for you; ask what you can do for your country."

— John F. Kennedy

| 1962 | 1962 | 1963 | 1963 |
|------|------|------|------|
| The Cuban Missile Crisis unfolds | The U.S. and Russia escalate nuclear weapons testing | Martin Luther King, Jr., makes his "I Have A Dream" speech | President Kennedy is assassinated |

# #36 Lyndon B. Johnson
## (1963 - 1969)

Lyndon B. Johnson (often referred to as LBJ) was born in Texas in 1908.  He graduated from college in 1930 and became a high school teacher.  A short time later, he entered politics and married Claudia Taylor.  Together, they had two children and worked to get LBJ elected to a U.S. House seat.  He won that election and several more!

During World War II, LBJ joined the Army; reported to General Douglas MacArthur; and was nearly shot down over the Pacific Ocean.  After the war, he became a U.S. Senator and a leader within the Democratic Party.  He then joined John F. Kennedy in making a run for the White House.  The election was close, but they won and LBJ became America's new vice president.

Born:  August 27, 1908
Died:  January 22, 1973

Lyndon B. Johnson became president after President Kennedy was killed.  He then won the Election of 1964.  In office, he saw passage of the Civil Rights Act of 1964 (which outlawed racial segregation in many areas); signed the Voting Rights Act (which outlawed voter discrimination); and declared a war on poverty.  These were all viewed as favorable to most people; however, after his popularity dwindled as a result of U.S. involvement in the Vietnam War and tax hikes, he didn't seek the presidency in 1968.

During World War II, Lyndon B. Johnson reported to General Douglas MacArthur (pictured here).

| 1963 | 1964 | 1964 | 1965 |
|------|------|------|------|
| Lyndon B. Johnson becomes president | The Beatles appear on the Ed Sullivan Show | Martin Luther King, Jr., receives the Nobel Peace Prize | U.S. combat troops arrive in Vietnam |

The Six-Day War in June of 1967 between Israel (backed by the U.S.) and its neighbors of Egypt, Jordan, and Syria (backed by Russia) nearly led to armed conflict between the U.S. and Russia. Both powers had a naval presence in the eastern Mediterranean and tensions were high, but the U.S. and Russia showed restraint by allowing the warring nations to fight it out for themselves.

The year 1968 marked a dark period in American history. On April 4th, civil rights leader Martin Luther King, Jr., (he was also a Baptist minister) was shot while standing on a hotel balcony and died in surgery afterwards. Two months later, civil rights activist and presidential hopeful Robert F. Kennedy was shot after giving a speech. Kennedy died the following day as a result of his wounds. Both King and Kennedy openly spoke about racial issues that were dividing the country, and many believe their deaths were the results of their calls for racial harmony.

Robert F. Kennedy

Robert F. Kennedy (the younger brother of President John F. Kennedy) was campaigning to become the Democratic Party's nominee for president when he was shot.

## PRESIDENT QUIZ

### WHO AM I?

1953 - 1961

Page 72

### TRIVIA

Who was president when the 1929 Stock Market Crash occurred?

Page 66

"We live in a world that has narrowed into a neighborhood before it has broadened into a brotherhood."
— Lyndon B. Johnson

| 1966 | 1967 | 1968 | 1968 |
|---|---|---|---|
| Bill Russell becomes first African-American head coach in NBA | Opposition to the Vietnam War grows | Martin Luther King, Jr., is assassinated | Robert F. Kennedy is assassinated |

# #37 Richard M. Nixon
## (1969 - 1974)

Richard M. Nixon was born in 1913 in California. After obtaining degrees from both Whittier College and Duke University, he became a lawyer. He married Thelma Ryan in 1938 and, when World War II started, joined the U.S. Navy where he obtained the rank of lieutenant commander.

After the war, Nixon returned to California and began his political career. He served as both a U.S. Representative and Senator for California, and then became Dwight D. Eisenhower's vice president for two terms. As vice president, Nixon undertook many foreign trips of goodwill to promote U.S. Cold War policies. In 1960, he took a big step and ran for president; however, he lost this contest to John F. Kennedy.

Born: January 9, 1913
Died: April 22, 1994

After Nixon sat out of the 1964 Election, he came back and won the 1968 and 1972 Presidential Elections. In office, he reduced American troop levels in Vietnam and airlifted weapons to Israel after it was attacked by Egypt and Syria. Shortly after Israel's victory, it came to light that President Nixon was involved in a cover-up of illegal activities known as Watergate. However, rather than face a trial, President Nixon resigned from office. He was the only president ever to resign.

President Nixon was the first president to visit China.

| 1969 | 1969 | 1970 | 1970 |
|------|------|------|------|
| Richard M. Nixon takes office | Neil Armstrong becomes the first man to walk on the moon | The U.S. Census counts 203 million Americans | First commercial flight of a Boeing 747 takes place |

Several men tied to President Nixon's administration were caught breaking into the Watergate complex trying to "tap" the phones of the Democratic National Committee. Later, President Nixon was caught in a series of lies trying to cover up his knowledge of the incident. So, rather than remaining president and possibly fighting the charges that were mounting against him, President Nixon resigned from office.

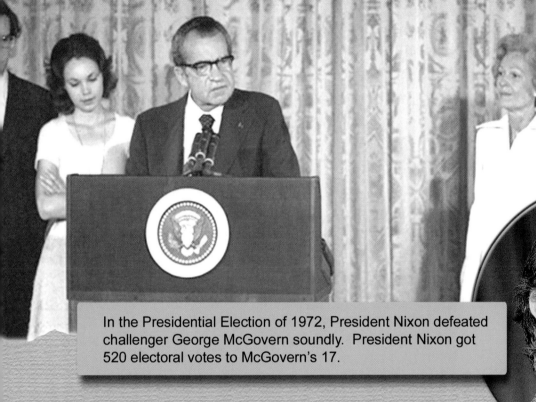

In the Presidential Election of 1972, President Nixon defeated challenger George McGovern soundly. President Nixon got 520 electoral votes to McGovern's 17.

George McGovern

## PRESIDENT QUIZ

### WHO AM I?

1869 - 1877

Page 40

### TRIVIA

Who was president during the Iran Hostage Crisis?

Page 82

"A man is not finished when he is defeated. He is finished when he quits."

— Richard M. Nixon

| 1971 | 1972 | 1973 | 1973 |
|------|------|------|------|
| China gets a seat on the United Nations Security Council | U.S. swimmer Mark Spitz wins seven Olympic gold medals | Gerald R. Ford becomes VP after Spiro Agnew resigns | Israel defeats Arab coalition in the Yom Kipper War |

# #38 Gerald R. Ford
## (1974 - 1977)

Gerald R. Ford was born in Nebraska in 1913. His birth name (which was changed following his mother's divorce and remarriage) was Leslie Lynch King, Junior. Ford became a star athlete; played football for the University of Michigan; and took a coaching job at Yale. A few years later, he was admitted to Yale Law School.

Born: July 14, 1913
Died: December 26, 2006

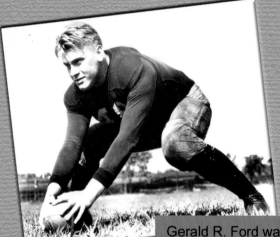

After graduating from law school, Ford returned to Michigan and opened a law practice in 1941. However, after Japan's attack on Pearl Harbor, he joined the naval reserves and fought in the Pacific. After the war, he married Elizabeth Warren and began a political career that took him to the U.S. House of Representatives. He later replaced Vice President Spiro Agnew who resigned from office.

Gerald R. Ford was a star athlete for the University of Michigan and helped its football team win national titles in 1932 and 1933.

Gerald R. Ford became president after President Nixon resigned in 1974. Nearly nine months into his presidency, North Vietnam conquered South Vietnam and U.S. involvement in the conflict essentially ended. Afterwards, President Ford pardoned President Nixon for his part in the Watergate scandal and many Americans were upset. When the Presidential Election of 1976 came about, President Ford was able to win the Republican Party's nomination, but he was unable to win the big one. When his term ended, President Ford retired from politics.

| 1974 | 1974 | 1975 | 1975 |
|------|------|------|------|
| Gerald R. Ford takes office | President Ford pardons Nixon of all crimes | American Bobby Fisher is stripped of his world chess title | Frank Robinson becomes MLB's first African-American manager |

On September 8, 1974, President Ford granted President Nixon a full pardon for any crimes that President Nixon might have committed while in office. Now, if you didn't know that a president could pardon someone of crimes, then you do now!

President Ford's decision upset many who thought that Nixon should have been put on trial for the Watergate Scandal mess.

----------

Did you know that President Ford is the only president not to be elected as either president or vice president?

As Speaker of the House of Representatives, he became vice president when Spiro Agnew resigned and, later, president when Richard Nixon resigned.

The Vietnam War came to an end when the South Vietnamese capital of Saigon was overrun by North Vietnamese forces in 1975. While troops from the North were moving in, the U.S. evacuated more than 7,000 American citizens and "at-risk" Vietnamese by helicopter.

North and South Vietnam became one nation under communist rule shortly after America's withdrawal.

## PRESIDENT QUIZ

### WHO AM I?

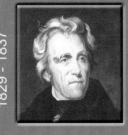

1829 - 1837

Page 18

### TRIVIA

Liberia named its capital in honor of this president.

Page 14

"A government big enough to give you everything you want is a government big enough to take from you everything you have."

— Gerald R. Ford

| 1975 | 1976 | 1976 | 1976 |
|------|------|------|------|
| The Vietnam War comes to an end | Barbara Walters becomes America's first female nightly news anchor | The U.S. Supreme Court upholds the death penalty | In television, Superstation WTBS goes national |

# #39 James E. Carter
## (1977 - 1981)

James Earl "Jimmy" Carter was born in 1924 in Georgia. He was a gifted student; excelled in basketball; and graduated from the U.S. Naval Academy in 1947. After serving six years in the navy, he returned to Georgia with his wife, Rosalynn, and took over his family's farm business. By 1970, he was considered a wealthy peanut farmer.

Carter's political career started in the Georgia Senate when racial segregation was the norm. In 1970, he ran for governor and refused to join the White Citizen's Council, a group favoring segregation. This angered many 'whites' in Georgia, but didn't stop Carter from winning the election. In office, he appointed many African-Americans to state offices. He later won the Democratic Party's nomination for president in 1976.

Born: October 1, 1924
Died:

Jimmy Carter won the Presidential Election of 1976. While in office, he worked to bring peace to various parts of the world; however, at home, an economic recession, high inflation, and an energy crisis hurt his popularity. Also, near the end of his term, fifty-two Americans were taken hostage in Iran for over a year and the U.S. Olympic team was ordered to boycott the 1980 Summer Olympics. These problems contributed to his landslide defeat in the 1980 Presidential Election.

JIMMY CARTER

PROJ

Jimmy Carter served in the U.S. Navy for six years and had the honor of having a Seawolf-class submarine named after him. The USS Jimmy Carter is one of a few ships in the U.S. Navy to have been named for a person who was alive at the time of the ship's naming.

| 1977 | 1977 | 1978 | 1978 |
|---|---|---|---|
| Jimmy Carter takes office | President Carter pardons almost all Vietnam draft evaders | Margaret Brewer becomes U.S. Marine's first female general | President Carter restores citizenship of Jefferson Davis |

The Iranian Hostage Crisis lasted from November 4, 1979, to January 20, 1981. It started when a group of militants and Islamist students stormed the U.S. Embassy in Iran and took American citizens hostage. During the 444-day crisis, negotiations to release the hostages took a turn for the worst when the U.S. military made a failed attempt to rescue the hostages. Operation "Eagle Claw" (as it was called) resulted in the deaths of eight American soldiers and the loss of a C-130 Hercules and a few helicopters. However, despite the failed rescue attempt, the U.S. was able to broker a deal with Iran to free the hostages. The fifty-two Americans were formally released on January 20, 1981, just twenty minutes after Ronald Reagan was sworn into office.

President-elect Ronald Reagan may have sped up the release of the hostages when he said that he would not pay "ransom for people who have been kidnapped by barbarians."

America celebrates the return of its freed hostages in 1981.

The "Miracle on Ice" occurred during the 1980 Winter Olympics Games in New York when the U.S. Hockey team (which consisted of college hockey players) defeated the mighty Soviet Union hockey team by a score of 4-3. Prior to the U.S. victory, the Soviets destroyed nearly everyone they faced, including a 6-0 route of the National Hockey League All-Star Team in an exhibition game!

## PRESIDENT QUIZ

### WHO AM I?

1969 - 1974

Page 78

### TRIVIA

Which president was Ronald Reagan's vice president?

Page 86

"War may sometimes be a necessary evil. But no matter how necessary, it is always an evil, never a good. We will not learn how to live together in peace by killing each other's children."

— Jimmy Carter

| 1979 | 1980 | 1980 | 1981 |
|------|------|------|------|
| Over 50 Americans are taken hostage in Iran | The U.S. Olympic hockey team defeats Russia | The U.S. Census counts 226 million Americans | The American hostages in Iran are released |

# #40 Ronald Reagan
## (1981 - 1989)

Ronald Wilson Reagan was born in 1911 in an Illinois apartment. He worked as a life guard, played sports, and was interested in acting. After a short stint as a radio sportscaster, he landed a contract with Warner Brothers studio and began a career in acting. Reagan later joined the military during World War II but could not serve overseas due to poor eyesight.

Born: February 6, 1911
Died: June 5, 2004

Ronald Reagan worked in radio and Hollywood before entering politics.

Ronald Reagan won the Presidential Elections of 1980 and 1984 in electoral vote landslides. In office, he worked to improve America's economy and declining status as a Superpower. He survived an assassination attempt; revamped the military; and escalated the Cold War with the Soviet Union. In the end, his "peace through strength" philosophy helped lead to the collapse of the Berlin Wall and the Soviet Union. After his second term ended, he retired from politics and returned to his ranch in California.

After the war, Reagan returned to the film industry and married Nancy Davis. He then turned his attention to politics and ran for governor of California. He won the election and served two terms before testing the waters for the presidency. In 1976, he challenged President Ford for the Republican Party's nomination and lost. Despite this setback, Reagan won more supporters and made a run to be the Republican Party's nominee four years later. This time around, he was successful.

Ronald Reagan was the oldest person to ever be elected president.

| 1981 | 1981 | 1982 | 1983 |
|------|------|------|------|
| Ronald Reagan takes office | President Reagan is shot and wounded in failed assassination attempt | Control of the Panama Canal is transferred to Panama | A national holiday is established to honor Martin Luther King, Jr. |

In 1987, President Reagan went to the Berlin Wall in Germany and challenged Soviet leader Mikhail Gorbachev to "tear down this wall."

In comparison to the decade before, American homes of the 1980s saw technological advancements in many areas. Computers, home video games, microwave ovens, VCRs, cable television, and cell phones became commonplace in many homes.

Although President Reagan and Pope John Paul II avoided being assassinated in the 1980s, Egyptian President Anwar Sadat; former Beatles star John Lennon; and Indian Prime Minister Indira Gandhi did not. All three were shot to death.

The Space Shuttle Challenger disaster occurred on January 28, 1986. Seven U.S. astronauts lost their lives that day.

## PRESIDENT QUIZ

### WHO AM I?

1901 – 1909

Page 56

### TRIVIA

Who was president during World War I?

Page 60

"Freedom is never more than one generation away from extinction. We didn't pass it to our children in the bloodstream. It must be fought for, protected, and handed on for them to do the same."

— Ronald Reagan

| 1984 | 1985 | 1986 | 1988 |
|------|------|------|------|
| The first planet outside our solar system is discovered | 248 U.S. soldiers die in airplane crash in Newfoundland | Seven U.S. astronauts die in Space Shuttle Challenger disaster | Nearly 2,000 pro-life protestors are arrested |

# George H. W. Bush
## (1989 - 1993)

George Herbert Walker Bush was born in Massachusetts in 1924. After the Japanese attack on Pearl Harbor, he postponed going to college and joined the U.S. Navy. He became the navy's youngest aviator at that time. After the war, he married Barbara Pierce, graduated from Yale University, and entered the oil business in Texas.

Born: June 12, 1924
Died:

By the age of 40, Bush was a millionaire and ready to enter politics. He won a seat to the U.S. House of Representatives in 1966 and later became the U.S. Ambassador to the United Nations. He then changed roles by becoming the Director of the CIA. and, in 1981, Ronald Reagan's vice president. The old navy pilot was certainly flying high!

After President Reagan served two terms, Bush ran for the presidency in 1988 and won. During his term, Iran invaded its neighbor, Kuwait. America and a coalition of allies then went to war to help small Kuwait and protect the world's oil supply. Iraq was easily defeated, but President Bush's popularity at home suffered when he broke a "no new tax" promise that he had made during his 1988 campaign for the White House. In siding with the Democratic Party and raising taxes, he angered many Republicans and was defeated by Bill Clinton, a Democrat.

Long before becoming president, George H. W. Bush was a fighter pilot for the U.S. Navy. He served during World War II and, at the age of eighteen, was the youngest naval aviator to that date.

| 1989 | 1989 | 1990 | 1990 |
|------|------|------|------|
| George H. W. Bush takes office | A major earthquake in California delays baseball's World Series | Douglas Wilder becomes first African-American to be elected governor | The U.S. Census counts 248 million Americans |

Douglas Wilder made history on November 8, 1989, by becoming the first African-American to be elected governor of a state. He defeated his challenger by less than half of a percent in the Virginia race and was sworn into office on January 13, 1990. In office, Governor Wilder focused on crime and gun control initiatives. He also ordered Virginia state agencies and universities to divest themselves of any investments in South Africa because of that nation's policy of apartheid. Because of Virginia's laws prohibiting successive gubernatorial terms, Wilder was unable to run for re-election in 1993.

Soon after Iraq invaded the small country of Kuwait in 1990, the United States joined a coalition of thirty-four nations and went to war against Iraq. The war (commonly referred to as the Gulf War, Operation Desert Storm, and the First Gulf War) ended in early 1991 after the coalition forces forced Iraq from Kuwait; destroyed much of Iraq's infrastructure and military forces; and imposed sanctions against Iraq.

The American-led coalition consisted of nearly 1,000,000 troops, 2,000 aircraft, and 3,000 tanks. In comparison, Iraq had 500,000 troops, 700 aircraft, and 4,500 tanks. After the fighting started, Iraqi forces were overwhelmed by superior weaponry and suffered more than 30,000 casualties. When compared to the less than 500 coalition casualties, this war was one of the most lopsided in history.

Soldiers from the United Kingdom advance into Kuwait in 1991.

## PRESIDENT QUIZ

### WHO AM I?

1977 - 1981

Page 82

### TRIVIA

Who became president after Abraham Lincoln was assassinated?

Page 38

"We don't want an America that is closed to the world. What we want is a world open to America."

— George H. W. Bush

| 1991 | 1991 | 1992 | 1992 |
|---|---|---|---|
| The U.S. and its allies attack Iraq for occupying Kuwait | The U.S. and its allies force Iraq to withdraw from Kuwait | VP Dan Quayle gets flak for spelling potato as "potatoe" | Four policemen indicted in the Rodney King beating case |

# #42    William J. Clinton
## (1993 - 2001)

William Jefferson "Bill" Clinton was born in Arkansas in 1946. As a student, he had many interests. He was an avid reader, a musician, and a student leader. While he was a member of Boys Nation, he visited the White House and met President John F. Kennedy. This encounter had a tremendous influence on young Clinton.

Clinton graduated from Yale Law School in 1973 and married Hillary Rodham two years later. He returned to Arkansas where he became the state's Attorney General and, later, it's governor! Clinton held this position for nearly twelve years and helped Arkansas improve its economy and educational system. In 1992, he ran for president as the Democratic Party's nominee.

Born: August 19, 1946
Died:

Bill Clinton won the Presidential Elections of 1992 and 1996. In office, he signed the Family and Medical leave Act of 1993; started the first official White House website; and helped fix a poor economy. In his second term, he was impeached based on allegations that he lied in a sworn deposition (i.e., perjury). He was found not guilty and served out his final term. When he left office, President Clinton was still popular and had a job approval rating of more than 70%.

The 1995 bombing of the Alfred P. Murrah Federal Building in Oklahoma City took the lives of 168 people, including 19 children under the age of six.

| 1993 | 1994 | 1995 | 1996 |
|------|------|------|------|
| Bill Clinton takes office | A Cessna airplane crashes on the White House lawn | Oklahoma City bombing kills 168 people at a federal building | One killed and many injured in bombing at the Atlanta Olympic Park |

In 1999, the United States and other members of NATO launched a military operation against the military forces of the Federal Republic of Yugoslavia. During this era, Yugoslavia was divided among several different ethnic groups; its government and military were supporting the ethnic cleansing of several minority groups; and a civil war was raging. To prevent further acts against humanity, President Clinton committed U.S. troops to force the Yugoslavian government to end its internal conflict. The strategy worked and U.N. peacekeeping forces soon entered the unstable nation to halt the ethnic unrest.

After serving as America's First Lady for eight years, Hillary Rodham Clinton began a political career. She became a U.S. Senator in 2001 and nearly the Democratic Party's candidate for president in 2008. In 2009, she gave up her Senate seat and became the Secretary of State in President Obama's Administration.

President Clinton's popularity showed when he easily defeated Republican Bob Dole and Reform candidate Ross Perot in the 1996 Presidential Election. With the win, Clinton became the first Democrat since President Franklin D. Roosevelt to be elected more than once.

## PRESIDENT QUIZ

### WHO AM I?

1981 - 1989

Page 84

### TRIVIA

Who was president when two atomic bombs were dropped on Japan?

Page 70

"America and Israel share a special bond. Our relationship is unique among all nations. Like America, Israel is a strong democracy, a symbol of freedom, and an oasis of liberty, a home to the oppressed and persecuted."

— Bill Clinton

| 1997 | 1998 | 1999 | 2000 |
|---|---|---|---|
| The U.N. pulls its inspection teams out of Iraq | Astronaut John Glenn, at the age of 77, returns to space | The U.S. Senate acquits President Clinton of lying under oath | The U.S. Census counts 281 million Americans |

# #43 George W. Bush
## (2001 - 2009)

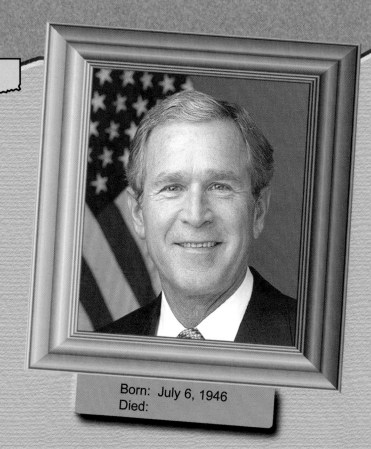

Born: July 6, 1946
Died:

George Walker Bush, the son of President George H. W. Bush, was born in Connecticut in 1946. After graduating from Yale University with a degree in history, he earned a masters degree at Harvard Business School; married Laura Welch; and returned to Texas, his childhood home. Here, he entered politics and the oil business.

After helping his father win the Presidential Election of 1988, George W. Bush bought a share in the Texas Rangers baseball franchise and then decided to run for governor of Texas. He won the election (focusing on tort reform, crime reduction, and education) and took office in 1995. He was re-elected to a second term in 1998 and turned his sights to the White House. In 2000, he became the Republican Party's nominee for president.

The U.S. and its allies invaded Afghanistan following the September 11, 2001, terrorist attacks.

George W. Bush became president after winning the Elections of 2000 and 2004. In office, he was faced with the worst terrorist acts on U.S. soil (the "9/11" attacks on New York's Twin Towers). This helped push the U.S. into wars in Afghanistan and Iraq. Many Americans became weary of the military's presence in these lands and President Bush's popularity declined. Then, after the Gulf of Mexico was hit by Hurricane Katrina, his popularity plummeted. After leaving office, President Bush retired from politics.

| 2001 | 2001 | 2001 | 2003 |
|---|---|---|---|
| George W. Bush takes office | Terrorists launch "9/11 Attacks" on the U.S. | The U.S. and its allies go to war in Afghanistan | The U.S. and its allies go to war in Iraq |

Following the September 11, 2001, terrorist attacks and the American-led invasion of Afghanistan, the U.S. and its allies went to war in Iraq under the name "Operation Iraqi Freedom". The war was a success. Suffering less than 200 casualties, America and its allies conquered Iraq swiftly and decisively. Iraq lost nearly 20,000 soldiers in the conflict.

Following its defeat, Iraq was allowed to form a new government. Saddam Hussein (pictured here), the former leader of Iraq, was hanged by Iraq's new government for crimes against humanity.

## PRESIDENT QUIZ

### WHO AM I?

1933 - 1945

Page 68

### TRIVIA

Who was president during the War of 1812?

Page 12

"After the chaos and carnage of September 11th, it is not enough to serve our enemies with legal papers."

— George W. Bush

| 2004 | 2005 | 2007 | 2008 |
|------|------|------|------|
| A tsunami kills more than 260,000 people in Asia and Africa | Hurricane Katrina slams New Orleans and the Gulf Coast | Nancy Pelosi becomes America's first female Speaker of the House | U.S. swimmer Michael Phelps wins eight Olympic gold medals |

# #44  Barack Obama
## (2009 - )

Barack Obama was born in Hawaii in 1961. In 1967, he moved with his family to Indonesia for four years. After returning to Hawaii, he attended a college "prep" school and graduated. He then went to Occidental College in Los Angeles before transferring to Columbia University where he obtained a B.A. in Political Science.

Born: August 4, 1961
Died:

In 1985, Obama began work as a director of a church-based community organization that set up a job training program, tutoring program, and tenants' right organization. Three years later, he entered Harvard Law School where he obtained a law degree. Afterwards, Obama began his political career by being elected to the Illinois state senate. A few years later, in 2004, he became one of that state's U.S. senators.

Barack Obama became the first African-American to be elected President. He took the oath of office on January 20, 2009.

Barack Obama won the Presidential Election of 2008, thus becoming the first African-American to win the presidency. In his first few days in office, he signed a bill that provided insurance coverage to four million children that were uninsured. He also enacted economic stimulus packages to help improve America's poor economy and is working on reforming American health care. The cost of such programs has led to the national debt ballooning to never-before-seen levels and has led to the emergence of the "Tea Party", a voter movement looking for a fiscally-sound, smaller federal government.

| 2009 | 2009 | 2009 | 2009 |
|------|------|------|------|
| Barack Obama takes office | Over 700 grass roots "Tea Party" protests occur in one month | The unemployment rate climbs above 10% | The U.S. sends more troops to Afghanistan |

Barack Obama's "hope" and "change" message proved successful for many Democrats at the polls. Not only did Obama defeat Republican Senator John McCain easily, but Democrats running for Congress also benefited. After the votes were counted, the Democratic Party saw its 236-199 lead in the House of Representatives increase to 257-178 and its slim 51-49 Senate lead balloon to 59-41. For the first time in decades, Democrats had control of the White House and both Houses of Congress!

———

Oh, how things can change. Exactly two years after gaining many Congressional seats, the Democratic Party suffered major setbacks.

When the votes were counted for the 2010 Congressional Elections, the Republican Party (with the help of the Tea Party movement) gained six seats in the Senate (cutting the Democratic advantage to 53-47) and even took control of the House!

The Republican Party selected Governor Sarah Palin of Alaska as its vice presidential nominee in 2008. Following the defeat of the McCain-Palin ticket, Palin stayed active in politics. She spoke at "Tea Party" rallies; voiced a conservative approach to federal spending; and, to many, is a viable presidential candidate for 2012. Palin also campaigned for many Republican females in 2010 as part of the "Pink Elephant Movement".

## PRESIDENT QUIZ

### WHO AM I?

1861 – 1865

Page 36

### TRIVIA

Which president was a hero of the Spanish-American War?

Page 56

"Change will not come if we wait for some other person or some other time. We are the ones we've been waiting for. We are the change that we seek."

— Barack Obama

**2010**
BP Oil Rig Disaster (oil pours into Gulf of Mexico for 3 months)

**2010**
18.9% of U.S. labor force is unemployed or under-employed

**2010**
Polls show many Americans are unhappy with government

**2010**
Many Democrats are defeated in mid-term elections

# Glossary of Terms

Congress:
> The U.S. Senate and the U.S. House of Representatives make up Congress. Together, they create bills that may become laws.

Election Day:
> For the president and vice president, election day occurs on the Tuesday after the first Monday in November within years that are evenly divisible by four. On this day, voters go to the polls. After a state tallies its votes, it selects electors to the electoral college that will eventually meet with other state electors to formally vote for the president and vice president.

Electoral College:
> This is a body of elected representatives (called electors) who formally elect the president and vice president. The number of electors each state has is equal to its number of U.S. Senators and Representatives. Oh, and Washington, D.C., gets a few too!

Electoral Votes:
> Each elector in the electoral college gets to cast one vote for the president and another for the vice president. In most cases, a state's electors cast all their votes for the same candidate(s).

First Lady:
> This is the president's wife. James Buchanan wasn't married when he was president, so the U.S. was without a First Lady during his term.

House of Representatives:
> This is one of the two Houses of the U.S. Congress. (The other House of Congress is called the Senate.) Its total number of representatives is currently limited to 435 and each representative serves a two-year term. Representatives are apportioned to each state based upon that state's population and elected by voters from within the states.

Impeachment:
> Impeachment is when formal charges are brought by members of legislature against a civil officer of government, including the president. If the charges are sufficient, a trial could take place and the individual could be removed from office.

Inauguration Day:
> This is the day that a newly-elected president takes office. Before 1933, Inauguration Day was March 4. With the passage of the 20th Amendment, it has occurred on January 20.

# Glossary of Terms

**Senate:**

This is one of the two Houses of the U.S. Congress. (The other House is called the House of Repesentatives.) Its total number of members is limited to two members (or senators) from each state (or 100). Each senator serves a six-year term and are elected by voters from the states.

**Speaker of the House:**

The Speaker of the House is the presiding officer of the U.S. House of Representatives. This person is chosen by the House of Representatives and is second in the United States presidential line of succession, just behind the vice president.

**President pro tempore:**

The president pro tempore is the highest-ranking senator in the U.S. Senate and presides over its sessions in the absence of the vice president (who is actually the President of the Senate). The president pro tempore is selected by members of the Senate and is third in the United States presidential line of succession, just behind the Speaker of the House of Representatives.

**Supreme Court:**

The U.S. Supreme Court is comprised of a Chief Justice and eight Associate Justices. These judges usually serve for life and hears many cases involving the law.

**Political Party:**

Political parties are formed when people with similar goals unite to elect individuals who share their viewpoints. There have been many polictical parties in U.S. history. The Democratic Party and the Republican Party are the two largest ones today.

**President:**

The president is the head of the Executive Branch of the U.S. Federal Government. (See page 4 for more information.)

**Veto:**

Veto is the Latin word for "I forbid." If the president doesn't want a bill to become law when it reaches his desk, he can veto it!

**Vice President:**

The vice president is first in the United States presidential line of succession. He is also president of the U.S. Senate.

## About the Author:

Joel King is a homeschool dad with a passion for writing Christian fiction and non-fiction and creating educational resources with unique twists. He loves to play games with his three boys and believes that children retain knowledge better when they are having fun. Joel has a B.S. degree in accounting from the University of Kentucky and works as a state auditor. He lives with his wife and three boys in western Kentucky where they have homeschooled their children for ten years.

## Also by Joel F. King:

Join us as we travel from coast to coast, learning about the 50 states! From the disappearance of England's first American settlement to California's population explosion of 1849, you'll experience the growth of a new nation. From Plymouth Rock to Pearl Harbor, you'll follow the course of American history and geography! Great for children 4th grade on up to adult!

ISBN#: 978-1-932786-26-2

Retail $18.95
80 glossy full-color pages.

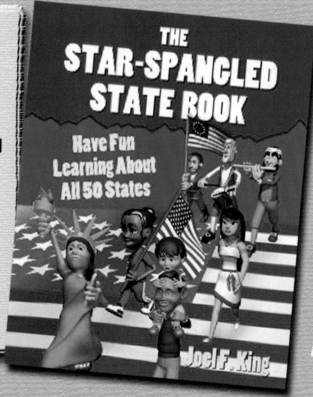

THE STAR-SPANGLED STATE BOOK

Have Fun Learning About All 50 States

Joel F. King